The Preservation and Restoration of
SOUND RECORDINGS

by Jerry McWilliams

American Association for State and Local History
Nashville

Library of Congress Cataloguing-in-Publication Data

McWilliams, Jerry, 1942-
    The preservation and restoration of sound recordings.

    Bibliography: p.
    Includes index.
    1. Sound recordings—Conservation and restoration.
I. Title.
TS2301.P3M22   621.389'32   79-17173
ISBN 0-910050-41-4

Photographs by Andrew Kudlacik

**Publication of this book was made possible in part by funds from the sale of the
Bicentennial State Histories, which were supported by the National Endowment for the
Humanities.**

For Iris and Carey
with love

Contents

Preface

Sound recordings as collectible items are a relatively recent phenomenon. The first sound recording process was not developed until 1877. The collection and preservation of written and printed materials had become established many hundreds of years prior to the introduction of the phonograph by Thomas Edison. Even with the availability of that radically new documentary technique, institutional collecting of sound recordings in the United States was slow to begin. The Library of Congress did not acquire its first sound recording until the early 1900s—a cylinder containing an address by Germany's Kaiser Wilhelm—and did not achieve significantly large holdings until the 1920s and '30s, with the gift of privately formed collections, including those of record companies. As late as World War II, few institutions were actively or seriously engaged in the collection of sound recordings. With the advent of the long-playing record in the early 1950s, however, the picture began to change. The collecting of sound recordings developed a broader base. Widespread availability of cassette technology in the 1960s served further to expand collecting. Today, sound recordings form an important part of the holdings not only of large research and university libraries but of state and local organizations, including archives, historical societies, museums, and corporate and other special libraries. There are also many large private collections of sound recordings.

Given the pervasive role that sound recordings now play in our society's cultural, economic, and historical workings, the numerous bases of sound recording collection activity, and the unique, often irreplaceable nature of many recordings, the means for the proper use, preservation, and—when necessary—restoration of sound recordings has become a growing concern.

Unfortunately, that was not always true. In part due to the spectacular nature of early sound recordings, manufacturers' minimal concern for durability, and the crass commercialism that characterized the American record business, librarians, archivists, and others in a position to collect and preserve were slow to take sound recordings seriously or to give them the kind of respect accorded to printed materials. Rare phonograph recordings, for example, have seldom been kept as carefully as rare books. Even as recently as 1971, a well-known authority on the preservation of library materials wrote:

> Sound recordings are made for play-back quality with emphasis on low manufacturing cost. Long life has never been a primary consideration. The short life expectancy and low resistance to degradation are properties incorporated in sound recording devices at the time of their manufacture and even unusual care cannot expand the normally expected life of a disc or tape.[1]

That essentially negative attitude is now changing, as more librarians, archivists, and curators become aware of preservation as a specialized and essential aspect of their professions, as they learn more about techniques and begin to perceive the over-all value of sound recordings to collections as well as potentially valuable objects in their own right.

A considerable body of literature has developed on the preservation and restoration of sound recordings in the past ten years. In addition, there have been a number of technical improvements in sound reproduction, particularly in disc playback, which have had a positive bearing on preservation. Together, these developments should convince most custodians of sound recordings of the success that can be achieved in their preservation. The fact is that many forms of sound recordings, when used carefully and stored under proper conditions, offer very long life with little deterioration in sound quality, either from inherent causes or through use—something that cannot be claimed for most modern printed materials. It is for precisely that reason that the preservation of sound recordings gains greater significance. Not only do sound recordings offer greater long-range stability than printed materials . . . their preservation and/or restoration can be more readily realized than can that of printed materials, which require enormously time-consuming and expensive measures, such as deacidification.

1. George D. Cunha, *Conservation of Library Materials: a Manual and Bibliography on the Care, Repair and Restoration of Library Materials,* 2d ed. (Metuchen, N.J.: Scarecrow Press, 1971), p. 41.

The present volume is an attempt to compress current thinking on the preservation and restoration of sound recordings into a practical, convenient handbook that can be used in setting up, maintaining, or improving a preservation program. It is intended to be helpful to both professional sound archivists and to those with less experience in the field. In view of the rapid rate with which sound recordings are being acquired by organizations other than sound archives, the needs of that group have been kept particularly in mind. The reader will find a theoretical discussion of the nature of recording media and ideal storage-and-use requirements for most kinds of sound recordings, as well as recommendations on how good storage-and-use conditions can be realized. A number of measures for restoring sound recordings that can be carried out firsthand will also be discussed, as well as the relationship of the Copyright Law of 1976 to preservation practice. Finally, there is a comprehensive bibliography for those wishing to pursue the subject further, a directory of manufacturers and suppliers for all products referred to in the text, and a list of major sound archives in the United States and Canada.

Sound recordings offer a fascinating, unique approach to historical and musical research. They should be given excellent care. The rewards of good care will become increasingly apparent in future years. I hope this book will help disseminate that idea and be of use to those wishing to implement it.

ACKNOWLEDGMENTS

I want to thank the following individuals for their time, interest, and encouragement in the research and preparation of this book: Professor Susan O. Thompson of the School of Library Service, Columbia University; Susan T. Sommer, Curator of the Toscanini Archives, Library and Museum of the Performing Arts, New York Public Library; Gary-Girard Gisondi and Sam Sanders of the Rodgers and Hammerstein Archives of Recorded Sound, Library and Museum of the Performing Arts, New York Public Library; Robert Carneal and Gerry Gibson of the Recorded Sound Section of the Library of Congress; Richard Warren of the Yale Collection of Historical Sound Recordings; and Jacqueline Harvey of the Audio Engineering Society. Thanks also to Andrew Kudlacik for photographic assistance and to M. Jerome Strong, M.D., whose electric typewriter proved invaluable.

Sound Recordings

1

History of Sound Recording

Since its inception in 1877, sound recording has passed through a number of technological stages. These developments have included the use of several distinctly different recording formats, such as cylinder, disc, and tape, as well as the use of different materials including wax, plastic, rubber, and metal. In addition, within each format, differing techniques have been used to register the sound. The sound archivist may therefore find himself custodian of a variety of different-sized, different-shaped objects, made of a wide range of materials and incorporating different technologies. These objects, in turn, will have particular requirements for use, storage, and restoration. This multiplicity of form complicates the preservation situation. Furthermore, it is not a static problem. Sound recording is in a state of active, even revolutionary, development. Several important technologies, involving lasers and electronic digital processing, are in the process of leaving the development stage and entering commercial application. These will spawn a new generation of equipment and vehicles for recorded information.

In considering the many kinds of objects to be dealt with, it will be helpful briefly to review the progress of sound recording from its beginnings in the late nineteenth century to the present day. That will establish a perspective for the development and use of different formats, materials, and technologies and provide a convenient background and frame of reference for the discussion of preservation and restoration to follow.

Disc and Cylinder Recording

The mid-nineteenth century witnessed a strong interest among scientists in the new field of acoustics. The most notable figure in acoustics at that time was Hermann von Helmholz, whose work established a theoretical basis for further investigation. Of immediate relevance to the history of sound recording was the work of French scientist Charles Cros. Cros sought a method of visualizing sound waves and, to that end, invented the phonautograph. The phonautograph was, in certain respects, prototypical of the modern phonograph. Sound waves activated a diaphragm that, in turn, caused a stylus to etch a visual record on a rotating disc covered with lampblack. The concept of the diaphragm, the stylus, and the rotating disc interlinking to record a continuous sonic event is the kernel of the idea that became the phonograph. Cros was apparently not interested in reproducing the sound for which he had made a record. Thomas Edison knew of the work of Helmholz and Cros.

Edison was a pragmatist; part of his greatness lay in an ability to grasp practical applications where others were content with theoretical models. Such was the case with the phonograph, a device whose time had come. Along with his pragmatic point of view, however, Edison possessed a restless imagination, a peculiar insight into the workings of electromechanical equipment, and he had the desire to perfect, which led him to original results. In developing the phonograph, Edison abandoned the rotating disc in favor of a rotating cylinder, a change that, to his mind, offered the possibility of superior results. In place of Cros's lampblack, which could record the impressions of a stylus but could never drive a stylus in the reproduction phase of the cycle, Edison employed tin foil. The foil was ductile enough to receive the stylus's impression, yet strong enough to drive it during playback. The stylus was moved across the cylinder by a screw feed. It is worth noting that, in Edison's original cylinder-recording process, the stylus—following the movement of the diaphragm—cut a vertically varying groove in the tin. The vertical, or hill-and-dale, cut was characteristically used on cylinder recordings throughout their manufacture.

The official date of the invention of the phonograph is July 18, 1877. It was demonstrated to the public at the offices of *Scientific American* in New York in that year. Original tin foils are now in the possession of the Smithsonian Institution.

From the beginning, preservation of the sonic content of these tin foil recordings was a problem. The foil was better for recording than for playback. Only a few playings were possible. Edison hoped to market the phonograph as a dictating machine, but there was little interest in it among businessmen. He temporarily shelved the project.

The idea, however, was abroad, and others took it up. Chichester A. Bell, a relative of Alexander Graham Bell, and Charles Sumner Tainter in 1885 applied for a patent on what they called a "gramophone"—a machine similar to Edison's, except that a wax-coated cardboard cylinder was substituted for the tin foil. The new material had two advantages over the old: sound quality was improved, and the recording was more durable. Competition reawakened Edison's interest. He subsequently developed a recording cylinder of solid wax, which was more stable than wax-covered cardboard.

From the beginning, those who worked in the phonograph field were attuned to the possible commercial exploitation of the machine. The lack of interest in 1877 caused Edison to turn his attentions elsewhere. As work continued and the wax cylinders were improved, public interest began to build. By 1890, the first commercial cylinders were on sale.

Cylinders, although technically well conceived, were not an ideal commercial vehicle, owing to a serious manufacturing limitation: in the early stages of their development, they could not be mass-produced. It was necessary to record each cylinder individually. Banks of machines were assembled to make recording sessions productive, but the problem was not fully resolved until later. In the meantime, a sizable advantage lay in developing a mass-producible sound recording. That feat was accomplished by Emile Berliner in 1887.

Berliner returned to the disc. His approach involved recording on a lampblack-covered surface. The impressions in the lampblack were fixed by an application of varnish and photoengraved on metal. Later, Berliner changed that method and began using, instead, a grease-covered zinc disc. After recording, the disc was dipped in acid and the resulting etching transferred to metal. The result, in either instance, was a stamping matrix that was used to stamp, or press, recordings in a system of mass-manufacture.

Berliner employed a lateral cutting technique. Subsequently, discs were cut in both lateral (side-to-side) and vertical (hill-and-

6 HISTORY OF SOUND RECORDING

dale) formats. The lateral cut eventually won out and is essentially the system used today.

The Berliner discs were pressed at first in vulcanized rubber, called vulcanite, which was advertised as being indestructible. It was found, however, that, as time passed, the rubber tended to flatten out. Attempts were made to find a better disc material. In 1897 shellac was introduced. Shellac, made from the excretions of the lac insect, had the desirable molding qualities and sufficient hardness to permit multiple playings.

The term *shellac,* as used in record manufacture, did not mean—at that time or subsequently—a disc made entirely of shellac. It was, rather, a convenient way of referring to a compound material. Shellac contained fillers, such as limestone or slate, pigment (usually carbon black), lubricants, such as zinc stearate, and binders and modifiers, such as Congo gum and vinsol. Similarly, wax cylinders were not composed entirely of wax, but were made of a mixture of substances designed to produce an economical yet technically acceptable recording.

The Duranoid Company of Newark, New Jersey, was one of the first large record-pressing companies (as distinguished from recording companies). The trade name *Duranoid*—the firm was originally a button manufacturer—was applied to the basic shellac formula used for 78-RPM recordings during the entire course of their manufacture, even as late as the 1950s, perhaps to imply a quality of the product. By modern standards, however, the durability of early discs, particularly in conjunction with the playback equipment of the day, was not good. The use of sharpened steel styluses operating at high tracking forces—nine ounces, compared with a modern cartridge tracking force of one gram—and nonstandard replacements could not have been beneficial. One early record manufacturer assured customers that if a needle became dull, "the broken-off tips of darning needles . . . are excellent substitutes."[1]

With two entirely different systems of sound recording on the market, backed by different commercial interests, competition was intense. The battle of rival technologies began, disc against

1. Roland Gelatt, *The Fabulous Phonograph* (Philadelphia: Lippincott, 1954), p. 55.

cylinder. Sonic quality (as distinguished from performance quality and general level of musical seriousness) was pursued on cylinders. A socialite and opera buff in New York, Gianni Bettini, produced what he called a "microphonograph," which had improved linkages between the diaphragm and the stylus. Edison, convinced of the superiority of cylinders, continued to work on wax formulations and in 1901 introduced the first hard-wax molded cylinder, the "Gold Mold." This device permitted cylinders to be mass-produced and greatly improved the hardness and uniformity of the recording surface. By 1903, the composition of Edison's wax cylinders included carnauba wax, lampblack, ceresin, stearic acid, lye, and sodium carbonate.

In 1900 the first wax disc was introduced. The wax disc gave sonic improvement over earlier discs and had a notably smoother, quieter surface. The most successful discs, up to that time, were the Caruso Milano recordings of 1902, on wax. The greater convenience of discs, the shrewdness of their exploiters and the generally more fashionable artists who recorded on discs (country and folk music was recorded, by and large, on cylinders) tipped the balance in their favor. Discs became the dominant force in the industry.

Technically, however, discs remained inferior. Edison continued work on cylinders, introducing, in 1908, the Amberol series with improved surfaces and grooving of two hundred lines per inch, which doubled the playing time to four minutes. In 1912 he came out with the Blue Amberols, which, it was claimed, could be played more than three thousand times without wear. The Blue Amberol cylinders outperformed any other medium of recorded sound then available. That achievement was due to several factors. First, the Blue Amberols had a smooth, hard, plasticlike surface unlike the gritty shellac disc that manufacturers had settled on. Second, Edison introduced a polished-diamond playback stylus greatly superior to the steel needles then used for discs. Third, the cylinder format had certain inherent advantages over the disc, the principal one being that groove velocity relative to the stylus remained constant. With discs, groove velocity continuously decreased as the stylus neared the center of the record, which meant that distortion increased near the center of discs.

As more manufacturers entered the burgeoning phonograph market, serious problems in standardization began to develop. To begin with, there were the rival formats, cylinder and disc, each requiring a specific type of playback apparatus. Then, cylinders and discs were manufactured in different sizes. Cylinders were made in 1 5/16-inch to 5-inch diameters, while discs were made in an even greater range of sizes. Different-sized discs, within limits, could be played on the same equipment, but cylinders of different diameters could not. A more serious problem was the great variety of rotational speeds at which discs were recorded. The original Berliner discs were recorded at 70 RPM, a compromise between playing time (lower speed) and sound quality (higher speed). Speeds from 74 RPM to 82 RPM were common, with some Pathés recorded as high as 90 RPM. This lack of standardization meant that the pitch and tempo of original performances were likely to undergo significant alteration as the discs were played on different machines. To a large extent, that problem was the result of spring-powered turntable drives. With the introduction of electric-drive motors, speeds became uniform. A final problem in standardization was whether discs were to be recorded from the outer rim inward, toward the center (outside-in) or from the center outward, toward the rim (inside-out). While most American commercial discs were recorded outside-in, some European-made discs, notably Pathé, were recorded inside-out. Many American instantaneous recordings, on the other hand, were recorded inside-out.

In the period from 1900 to World War I, the American record industry was marked by intense competition, not only between advocates of the disc and the cylinder, but between rival commercial groups, especially Victor and Columbia. At the same time, it was a period of great growth in the sales of both phonograph equipment and records and witnessed the emergence of Victor and Columbia as million-dollar corporations. Edison's continuing work on the cylinder and the introduction of the laminated disc were probably the main technical developments at that time.

The laminated disc was brought out by Columbia in 1906, supposedly with the assistance of Guglielmo Marconi. In the lamination process, a heavy kraft-paper central core was coated with shellac compound. This process had several advantages. It meant that less shellac could be used and that it was therefore economically possible to use a finer quality of shellac, producing a quieter surface. The famous Edison Diamond Disc was a laminated record of very high quality. Laminated records present special preservation problems because of the unstable nature of the paper core.

In the 1920s, the record industry went into a slump due to the introduction of an entirely new form of entertainment: radio. The great popularity of the new medium convinced some record manufacturers that the end was at hand. However, vacuum-tube amplifer technology, developed for radio transmission, was to provide the phonograph with its next major technical breakthrough.

Prior to 1925, all recording had been accomplished acoustically. In that process, it was the physical power of vibrating air, set in motion by the performers, concentrated by the familiar horn device, and converted to mechanical vibration by the diaphragm, that drove the cutting stylus. This method had limitations, including a lack of sensitivity and restricted frequency response. Practically, that meant that only sonic information produced at a high-decibel level and within a limited range could be effectively recorded. It was no accident that the recordings of Enrico Caruso were successful—the tenor's vocal power and range coincided with the requirements of acoustic recording. It was virtually impossible, however, to make a good acoustic recording of a symphony orchestra.

For that reason, investigation began in 1919 at the Bell Laboratories into the possibility of achieving electrical sound recording. The pioneering work was done by Joseph P. Maxwell and Henry C. Harrison. The application of the vacuum-tube amplifier to the disc-recording process, although theoretically feasible, involved working out complex engineering problems. When the system was perfected, it was demonstrated to major record manufacturers who, with their well-established conservatism, were initially unenthusiastic. The overwhelming advantages of the electrical recording system, however, eventually forced manufacturers to adopt it. The first commercial electrical recordings were issued by Victor and Columbia in 1925.

In the electrical system—basically the one used today in the making of disc masters—a microphone picks up the sound waves and converts them to electrical signals. These are then amplified by an electronic circuit, and the resulting high-powered signals are used to drive an electromagnetic cutting stylus. A great deal more sonic information could be gathered and recorded with microphones than with the acoustic horn. Frequency response and dynamic range were significantly increased, even in the early stages of the system's development.

Electrical recording, for all its advantages, was not without problems. The increased range of the equipment meant that recording sessions had to be conducted more carefully to avoid picking up background noise. Also, the increased range meant that distortion would be more noticeable. The use of lateral cutting, the disc format, and magnetic cutting equipment together created certain inherent problems that, in order to be controlled, required the application of different types of equalization. Equalization is an emphasizing or de-emphasizing of particular parts of the frequency spectrum during recording and playback to provide linear reproduction. The two main types of equalization applied were diameter equalization, to compensate for the changes in groove velocity from outside to inside the disc, and frequency-response equalization, to compensate for the effects of magnetic transducers, which are inherently nonlinear. A third type of equalization was applied by manufacturers to achieve a "house" sound. That was a less prominent problem during the days of 78-RPM recordings than it became with the introduction of long-playing discs.

As with the problem of turntable speed, equalization was not uniform. Each manufacturer had a favored equalization practice. Sound archivists, desiring to recreate the sound of original performances, have gone to considerable lengths to establish the past equalization procedures of record manufacturers. An industrywide standard was not agreed upon until 1953, with the adoption of the Recording Industry Association of America (RIAA) equalization curve for frequency-response equalization. Diameter equalization is still applied or not applied by manufacturers, according to house preference, although RIAA has set an inner diameter beyond which recording should not take place. Exaggerated "house" sounds persist.

Around 1929 Edison halted his production of all sound recordings. Cylinder sales had decreased, and it was clear that discs had become the established industry medium. From 1929 until the introduction of other media after World War II, all commercially produced sound recordings were issued in the laterally cut, outside-to-inside shellac-disc format. The commercial sphere, however, was not the only area where sound recording was taking place. Widespread availability of equipment and the flexibility of the electrical-recording process had combined to make noncommercial recording important by the 1930s. That was particularly true in the fields of ethnomusicology, conference documentation, and home recording. Sound recordings also began to be made in this period by radio stations and motion picture companies. In these areas, where recordings were not released for public sale, convenience and speed were important. To that end, several new materials were introduced for disc recording, including cellulose acetate and cellulose nitrate. Disc recordings made on these and certain other substances are referred to as "instantaneous."

In the instantaneous-recording process, the acetate or nitrate lacquer is used to coat a thin disc, usually—though not always—made of aluminum. The recording stylus cuts the sonic information into the soft coating, using the electrical process. When the recording session is complete, a finished disc is ready for playback. This process differed from commercial methods, where a master was cut (originally in soft wax, but subsequently in nitrate); the master was metal-plated and then used to produce a solid metal "mother," which in turn was used to produce metal stamping matrices.

The instantaneous process, while it could produce recordings of high quality, had one main drawback: the acetate or nitrate surfaces were soft and could be played only a few times before significant deterioration occurred. Instantaneous recordings, for that and other reasons, present major preservation and use problems.

Materials other than cellulose acetate and nitrate were used to produce field recordings. The Library of Congress, for example, has a collection of field recordings made on zinc discs. Diameters of instantaneous discs correspond, for the most part, to commercially produced discs, with the exception of discs made by radio stations and recordings of conferences and speeches, which typically employed 16-inch transcription discs. Most instantaneous recordings were made at a nominal 78 RPM.

Little significant progress was made in disc-recording technology during the 1930s and '40s in the United States. In Europe, particularly in England and Germany, sound quality of 78-RPM recordings was improved on labels such as London (with its "Full-

Frequency Range Recordings") and EMI, but no major improvement occurred until the introduction of the long-playing record by Columbia on June 21, 1948.

The concept of using lower record speeds to increase playing time dates to at least 1931, when RCA Victor demonstrated a long-playing disc. Edison also experimented with long-playing, low-speed discs. The technique was used in a number of commercial motion-picture sound systems. In fact, the speed of 33⅓ RPM, the current industry standard, was developed from a need to synchronize disc playback time with one reel of motion-picture film. It was found that a 20-inch diameter disc played at 33⅓ RPM would synchronize well with one reel of film and provide the necessary sound quality.

The recording industry did not return to the idea of using lower record speeds until 1944, when Columbia began its own development program under the direction of the late Peter Goldmark. The Columbia system involved not only the use of slower speeds, but used finer grooving, as well. The standard grooving of 78-RPM records varied from 96 lines to 125 lines per inch. The Columbia system of microgrooves varied from 250 lines to 400 lines per inch. Due to the gritty nature of shellac surfaces, their use for such narrow grooving would have been impractical. Although polymerized vinyl chloride had been used in the manufacture of discs by Western Electric, RCA, and Muzak before World War II, it was the war, with its great development of plastics chemistry and molding techniques, and the significant increase in shellac prices, that made the use of vinyl practical, if not essential.

As with shellac and wax records, the "vinyl" long-playing record has never consisted of merely vinyl chloride, but is a compound of polymerized vinyl chloride, plasticizer (polyvinyl acetate), filler, pigment, stabilizers, and antistatic substances.

The introduction of the long-playing record ushered in a major phase in the history of the American recording industry. It was, perhaps, the most important innovation since the original development of sound recording, because it had the effect of making sound recordings universally available—and an inherent part of American culture.

Long-playing records proved popular for several reasons. First, the greater playing time corresponded better to musical units of length and reduced the bulk of long recordings. Second, the sonic quality of the discs was superior to the best 78s, with quieter surfaces and still greater frequency response and dynamic range. Third, the LPs were unbreakable and offered much greater resistance to wear, when used on proper equipment, than 78s.

In 1950, RCA Victor brought out the 45-RPM "Extended-Play" disc as a counter-ploy to Columbia's long-playing discs. Early 45s were made of vinyl, but as the medium gained acceptance in the burgeoning youth market of the 1950s, polystyrene was introduced—it lent itself to rapid, inexpensive injection-molding techniques. While the 45-RPM microgroove format has theoretical advantages over its 33⅓-RPM counterpart, these were not taken advantage of until recently, and the 45 must be viewed primarily as a commercial tactic. In that, it has been quite successful. Serious music was never extensively recorded on 45s. They became, instead, the standard format for popular-music "singles." There is intense interest among private collectors today in 45s, particularly those from the 1950s. Some command high prices.

The most recent important development in the history of disc technology was the introduction of stereophonic recording in the late 1950s. Again, the idea was not new. Stereophonic sound—the provision of two or more independent simultaneous sound channels—had been proposed for motion-picture sound systems in the early 1930s. The present-day 45°/45° system of two-channel disc recording was described in 1931. The development of the long-playing record was an important step in making stereophonic recording a practical reality. There would have been little advantage to stereophonic reproduction, given the noisy surfaces of shellac discs. Walt Disney's motion picture *Fantasia*, with its spectacular sonic effects made possible by three-channel sound, helped increase popular awareness of stereophonic recording. The advent of solid-state electronic devices also helped make stereo a commercial reality by lowering the cost of amplification systems.

Decca Records (England) was among the pioneer companies urging the industry to adopt stereo recording. Decca had done considerable developmental work on a lateral-vertical cutting system. A committee set up by the RIAA conducted tests and concluded that the 45°/45° lateral-cutting system developed by Charles C. Davis of Westrex offered best results. That system was adopted as the standard of the international recording industry in March 1958, after a series of unusually co-operative meetings. The problem of standardization never arose. The first commercial stereo recordings using this system were issued later that year.

More recent developments in disc technology include the quadraphonic disc, introduced in the late 1960s, and direct-to-disc recording—a rebirth of the original disc-recording technique, which began to be marketed in the mid-1970s.

For quadraphonic discs, four independent sound channels are recorded, usually from two front and two rear sound sources. These are then encoded in such a way that the information can be recorded in two stereo channels. In order to retrieve the four channels, a complementary decoding process takes place during playback. Although many quadraphonic recordings have been released, the system has not yet become popular. The expense of providing two additional amplifiers and speakers is one reason. Another is that, to many people, the system seems to offer little sonic advantage over two-channel stereo. More seriously, there are several distinctly different, incompatible coding systems. These include SQ, QS, and CD-4. The industry has not yet standardized on that and the outlook for standardization is not good. Fortunately, the industry did take care to make quadraphonic discs compatible with stereo record-playing equipment. An archive collecting these recordings need not equip itself with special playback equipment, although failure to do so may gradually degrade third- and fourth-channel information if the discs are played frequently.

In direct-to-disc recording, the intermediate taping stages are eliminated, thereby returning, in one sense, to the form of disc recording in use before World War II. Other procedures used by standard record manufacturers to "improve" their recordings are also eliminated. The argument is that multichannel taping, mixdown, and forms of signal processing such as gain-riding and special equalization degrade sonic quality. The results in some cases have been impressive. Preservation requirements for direct-to-disc recordings are no different from requirements for other vinyl LPs. Direct-to-disc recordings have been issued in 33⅓ and 45 RPM speeds.

Tape Recording

Discs were the primary medium for sound recording in the United States through World War II. That situation dramatically changed in the postwar period with the importation of magnetic tape recording from Germany. During the war, the Allies were puzzled by full-length, apparently live symphonic broadcasts from Germany, because they knew that many concert halls and broadcast studios had been destroyed. When occupation forces reached Hamburg, they discovered the answer to this puzzle—a fully developed magnetic recording system installed in the studios of the German National Radio. The system made possible long-duration sound recordings of a quality far greater than had been obtained on discs.

Magnetic sound recording was first demonstrated by Vladimir Poulsen in 1899, although it had been theoretically described as early as 1888 by Oberlin Smith. Poulsen was a Danish experimenter and inventor who made important contributions to radio broadcasting. In Poulsen's system, a signal was taken from a standard telephone transmitter and applied through an electromagnetic head to a steel wire moving at seven feet per second. The device was called a telegraphone. The system was expensive, required long rewinding time, and duplicates could not be made. A further disadvantage was that the level of reproduced sound was low, requiring the use of earphones. The telegraphone produced some interest in the United States, but it was of an academic nature.

Dr. Lee De Forest, inventor of the vacuum-tube amplifier, in 1912 applied an electronic amplifier to the telegraphone system, but this potentially important marriage of technologies was without issue. In 1921 two American scientists, W. L. Carlson and G. W. Carpenter, developed the concept of alternating-current bias, essential for high-quality magnetic recording, but that discovery went unnoticed for a number of years. A patent was issued to Carpenter and Carlson in 1927, at which point what little American work had been done in magnetic recording came to an end.

Germany emerged as the main center for magnetic-recording research, largely as a result of the work of one man, Kurt Stille.

Stille worked on a method of sound recording on steel bands. His procedure achieved some success in the broadcasting industry, although the system was cumbersome due to the size and weight of the bands. Another German by the name of Pfleumer originated the concept of a magnetic coating on plastic or paper tape. In 1931, Allgemeine Elektrizitäts-Gesellschaft took over the idea and by November 19, 1936, was able to make the first tape recording of a symphony orchestra. The introduction of the German machines here in 1946 by John Mullin and the subsequent formation of the Ampex Corporation in 1948 brought about the almost universal adoption of magnetic recording by the recording and broadcasting industry.

Tape recording, with its great improvement in frequency response and dynamic range, its capability to produce long, uninterrupted recordings, its relatively lower noise, and its ability to be edited, became the first choice for professional recording. Low-priced units were introduced in this country beginning around 1953.

An alternate form of magnetic recording on wire was developed in the United States during the Second World War. From about 1945 to 1955, wire recording enjoyed a brief popularity, particularly in the consumer market. Many amateur recordings from that period will be found on wire. Wire recording was supplanted by tape, due to the lower sound quality available on wire and the many problems associated with wire transport mechanisms. Wire recordings today present serious problems of preservation, use, and restoration.

Magnetic recording, whether on wire or tape, operates on the principle that sound waves, converted to a changing electromagnetic field by microphones, amplifiers, and an inductive coil (or head), will magnetize iron oxide particles on a moving tape (or steel wire or band) in a manner analogous to the original sound. These magnetized particles (called domaines), when moved past a receptor head, will create electrical signals that can be converted back to the original sound. Although the principle is simple, several important signal-processing stages are required to ensure linear, distortion-free results. These include the application of a high-frequency current (bias) and several stages of equalization, one in recording and another in playback.

In addition to an inherent nonlinearity, the iron oxide medium has other drawbacks. The main one is noise. While tape is noticeably free of the kind of crackle, popping, and groove-wall noise associated with discs, it has a form of noise of its own, called *hiss*. Until recently, professionals have lowered tape hiss by recording at high tape speeds. Within the past ten years, however, two successful commercial noise-reduction systems have come into use. They are the Dolby System and **dbx**.

Perhaps due to the late arrival of magnetic tape recording in the United States, problems in standardization for it were very largely avoided. For example, professional recording in this country has almost always been at 30 inches or 15 inches per second (IPS) tape speed, on ¼-inch, ½-inch, 1-inch, or 2-inch tape width (until the last ten years, mostly ¼-inch), on 10½-inch reels and using ½-track heads (the entire width of a ¼-inch tape is full track). Amateur recording has been predominantly at 7½ or 3¾ IPS, or ¼-inch tape, using ½- or ¼-track heads and 7-inch and 5-inch reels. The National Association of Broadcasters (NAB) developed an extensive series of standards for magnetic tape recording, including the highly important equalization standard. These standards were most recently codified in 1966.

While format and equalization have remained relatively constant, there have been significant changes in the makeup of the tape itself. Early tapes used a magnetic coating on a paper base. Paper proved unsatisfactory because of its high noise (due to its relatively rough surface) and dimensional instability. Cellulose acetate was next used as a base. Many recordings made through the 1950s, even professional ones, were on acetate-base tape. Acetate tapes are still manufactured. It has been found, however, that the material will become brittle and decompose with time. Mylar-base tape was introduced in the 1950s and is now the standard type of tape for professional and most amateur work.

Tapes have been manufactured in various thicknesses, chiefly .5 mil, 1.0 mil, and 1.5 mil (a mil is one-thousandth of an inch). Professional recording is customarily done on 1.5-mil tape. One-mil tape is more commonly found among amateur recordings.

There have been changes in the iron-oxide magnetic coatings over the years. Improvements have occurred in the purity and consistency of coatings, as well as their composition. Chromium oxide has been used as a coating, both by itself and with iron oxide. This technique has extended the high-frequency response of tapes. A new generation of pure-metal particle coatings is about to appear. The preservation requirements for tapes have, in the past, been largely determined by the thickness and nature of the base.

As tape-recording technology developed in sophistication during the 1960s, several important developments took place. The first was the advent of multitrack recording, and the other was the introduction of the cassette format.

Multitrack recording, or the recording of two or more channels of sound simultaneously, was available in the mid-1950s to late 1950s for stereophonic recording. For professional applications, this typically meant two channels recording ½-track on ¼-inch tape, and for amateur recording, two channels at ¼-track on ¼-inch tape. With the ability to produce high-precision recording heads, it became possible to stack the heads vertically into clusters of 4, 8, 16, or 32 heads. This entailed the use of wider tapes, such as ½-inch, 1-inch, and 2-inch. Multitrack recording became popular among professionals, particularly for recording popular music and large symphonic works. It meant that multiple microphones could be used and a large number of independent channels mixed down to produce a master two-channel version. The mix-down process allowed engineers to achieve the kind of balance they sought with maximum convenience. In the case of popular music, separate parts could be recorded at different times and places. Tapes in multitrack format are beginning to find their way into recorded sound collections, and, while their preservation requirements are identical to other tape formats, the ability to retrieve the sonic information on them is dependent on having the proper professional equipment, as well as mix-down facilities and some concept of what the original composers, arrangers, performers, and engineers intended when the parts were recorded. Multitrack, multimicrophone techniques have come under attack recently as producing unnatural-sounding recordings.

The tape cassette, developed by the Dutch Philips Company, grew out of the desire to reduce the size and weight of recording equipment and to overcome consumer resistance to prerecorded tapes (the commercial production of prerecorded reel-to-reel tapes has never been successful). The cassette format, based on improved magnetic-head technology and good iron-oxide coatings, has come to play a dominant role in the consumer, or nonprofessional, tape industry. A great number of sound recordings are made on cassettes, not only for private use, but also by oral history programs, museums, and in the recording of conferences, meetings, musical events, and lectures.

Cassettes present a number of special problems in preservation, use, and restoration. These arise from the use of very thin and narrow tape, low tape speed (1⅞ IPS), the nonstandard internal construction of the cassette container and the frequently poor quality of equipment used to make recordings. Sound archives and music libraries find that they must deal with ever-increasing numbers of cassettes. This is accounted for by the great convenience of that form of recording.

In an attempt to overcome the sonic restrictions of the cassette—limited frequency-response, wow and flutter (instability in tape speed resulting in audible variations in pitch), low headroom (limited dynamic range), and elevated hiss levels—the Japanese tape-recorder industry has introduced the Elcaset, essentially a scaled-up version of the compact cassette. It uses ¼-inch tape in place of the compact's ⅛-inch and operates at a speed of 3¾ IPS. Special equipment is required to record and play the Elcaset. It is unclear whether this form of recording will become general. At present, it would seem not. The advantage of better sound quality is probably offset by the Elcaset's greater size.

Cassette equipment is produced in both monophonic and stereophonic types. Monophonic equipment is used primarily for recording speech. It usually has a low signal-to-noise ratio (that is, a high level of tape hiss). In order to reduce hiss in stereo equipment, Dolby noise-reduction circuitry is built into many recorders.

Digital Sound Recording

It was inevitable that the revolution in digital electronic data processing would affect the field of sound recording. Electronic digital processing of sound, until recently confined to the laboratory, has now become a practical reality. The sound-recording industry, in all probability, will convert to digital recording entirely. Among pioneering work done in that area was the digital reprocessing of old Caruso discs by the Soundstream Corporation. Soundstream also developed one of the earliest operational digital tape recorders. Digital recording has been made a practical success by the work of leading Japanese audio equipment manufacturers.

Digital sound recording operates on the principle that sound waves, once converted to electrical signals (analog form), may be electronically processed (sampled) and converted into digital information, which can then be recorded onto tape or disc. The sampling rate is kept sufficiently high to ensure that the process—high-speed but not continuous—does not lose audible sonic information. Once in digital form, the information can be far more effectively recorded than when in analog (conventional) form. Playback involves a complementary decoding.

Digitally encoded discs are produced by a laser that cuts precisely measured pits into a rapidly rotating disc (1,800 RPM). The pits are also read by laser. Discs are pressed in the same way that analog records are manufactured. Currently, they contain about the same amount of recording time as analog discs, but that figure is expected to increase significantly in the next few years. One of the advantages of using lasers is that no object ever makes physical contact with the vinyl surface of the disc, and hence wear is eliminated. Frequency response and dynamic range are greatly extended, while other forms of distortion peculiar to discs are eliminated. Noise becomes essentially nonexistent. Mitsubishi and TEAC, working together with Tokyo Denka, are the backers of this system.

Similar advantages are claimed for digital tape recording. This is physically similar to analog tape recording, in that a magnetic head makes contact with a moving tape to impart the sonic information, in this instance digitally encoded. In some systems a fixed head is used and in others it is a rotating type (as in video recorders). Principal developers in the field are Minnesota Mining and Manufacturing/British Broadcasting Company (3M/BBC), Japan Victor Corporation (JVC), Soundstream, Technics, and Sony. Sony, JVC, and Technics, developers of rotating-head systems, plan to market adaptor units that will allow the use of their video recorders to record sound digitally.

The major Japanese firms have developed systems that are not mutually compatible. The standardization problem may recur here. The Audio Engineering Society, the pre-eminent professional society in its field in the United States, has set up a Digital Audio Standards Committee to try to cope with the situation. Archivists collecting digitally encoded recordings will have to exercise care to note the particular type of system on which the recordings were made. Ideally, the full details of each recording system should be kept on hand in a technical file.

The equipment necessary for recording and playing back digitally encoded tapes and discs is, at present, expensive. Eventually, there should be a drop in price as standards are chosen and the industry tools up for this new technology. Sound archives should, in the long run, benefit from digital sound recording—it appears to eliminate almost all of the problems associated with analog recording.

2

Preservation of Sound Recordings

To preserve means "to cause to continue or last indefinitely" and "to keep or save from injury or destruction." Part of the purpose of any collection of documentary or published materials, whether they be sound recordings, books, or photographs, is to save these items from the harm that might come to them in uncaring or unskilled hands. In that respect, a collection of sound recordings is no different from any other archive. Sound recordings, however, due to the substances of their manufacture, as well as their inherent nature and method of use, have preservation requirements somewhat broader than those for other kinds of materials. Anyone who proposes to deal with them will be accepting an expanded definition of the concept of preservation.

Central to that idea is the fact that the sound archivist, or any other individual working with a collection of recordings, is responsible not only for the classification, arrangement, and safety of these articles, but also, upon patron request, for the recreation of the music, speech, or other information recorded on them. To put it another way, the sound archivist is responsible for the sound recording as physical object, as well as for its sonic content.

Preservation activities therefore break down into two main categories. Preservation of the physical object requires that the proper storage conditions be maintained and that appropriate methods of playback be employed. Preservation of the sonic content of a sound recording will almost invariably involve transferring the content from a fragile or decomposing medium to a stable one, such as reel-to-reel tape.

These combined responsibilities are not shared by curators of rare books or music manuscripts, for example, who concern themselves primarily with the organization and physical safety of their collections, or in any situation where the appreciation and use of materials is accomplished by the patron directly. The sound recording, however, although we do not think of it this way, is an extension of a machine, a part designed to fit into a large, often highly complex mechanical or electro-mechanical system. The optimal function of that system has a vital bearing on the retrieval of sonic content and on the life expectancy of the sound recording itself. Anyone who deals with sound recordings, therefore, must consider their welfare not just as static objects on a shelf, but as objects that, at one point or another, enter into a dynamic process. The static situation is represented by *storage* requirements and the dynamic by *playback* requirements.

Storage

Storage is the single most important archival function. In the case of archives or libraries with limited funds, provision of proper storage conditions may be the only function that can be realistically carried out. When storage conditions are ideal—and in general that is not too difficult to arrange—many types of sound recordings will last indefinitely, including all long-playing discs, most shellac discs, and most mylar-base reel-to-reel tapes. Fortunately, good storage conditions for sound recordings are similar to good conditions for books and thus may already prevail in libraries and other institutions where sound recordings are housed.

One reason for the similarity in storage requirements between sound recordings and printed materials is that many kinds of sound recordings are made from the same or similar substances as printed items. Vinyl, shellac, and paper all consist primarily of polymerized organic molecules. In polymerization, molecules link together to form long chains that, in turn, are often cross-linked to each other. This produces a strong, flexible material. In paper, molecules of cellulose are tied together and in discs, shellac or vinyl chloride. Identical substances are used in the manufacture of both sound recordings and books. For example, lampblack—a form of powdered carbon—is used to make records black (polyvinyl chloride is colorless) and to make printer's ink black. Wood pulp is used to make paper and was sometimes used as a filler for shellac discs in the form of wood flour. Cellulose, derived from wood, is the basic building block for cellulose acetate and nitrate, used in making discs for instantaneous recording and blanks for disc masters. Cellulose is, at the same time, the basis for paper manufacture. In addition, certain types of fine particulate matter, such as calcium carbonate, are used as filler in both disc and paper manufacture.

Aside from these internal similarities, sound recordings are often packaged and stored in intimate contact with paper, which links their treatment together to some extent. Many cylinders and laminated discs had paper cores, while 78s and 45s were packaged directly in paper. Long-playing discs have paper dust jackets and many LPs now have glassine (a form of paper) inner liners. Modern magnetic tape, although normally sold in paper boxes, is typically wound on plastic or metal reels and is less tied to paper chemistry than other recording media. However, early magnetic tapes were produced on both cellulose acetate and paper bases.

General Storage Requirements

The fundamental environmental requirement for printed materials and sound recordings alike is stable temperature and humidity. Organic materials, particularly those closely derived from natural products, are quite responsive to changes in temperature and humidity. Changes in moisture content will cause them to swell or shrink as humidity rises and falls. Changes in temperature will also cause expansion and contraction, often of significant proportions. Cycling of environmental conditions, causing repeated expansion and contraction of items in storage, is harmful in the long run. It will introduce stresses that lead eventually to deformation and actual breakage, resulting in distortion or complete loss of sonic content.

In addition to relative environmental stability, organically derived materials require moderate levels of absolute temperature and humidity. High temperature and humidity encourage fungal attack on these items and accelerate internal chemical reactions that may lead to decomposition. While fungi and various airborne molds exist in all environments, they need certain conditions in order to develop to the point where they pose a problem. When temperature and humidity are high, fungi will literally eat compounds like shellac, vinyl chloride, and wax. Pitting is left where that has occurred. Micro-organisms will also produce a physical build-up as a result of the colonies in which they live.

Many organic materials are host to continuous internal chemical reactions of a self-destructive nature. These are called oxidation-reduction reactions. They are fueled by the presence of oxygen in the atmosphere and available hydrogen in the material itself. Oxidation-reduction reactions result in the production of acid that further attacks the original material. These reactions take place at a rate geometrically proportional to temperature. For every increase in temperature of ten degrees Fahrenheit, the reaction speed approximately doubles, this according to Arrhenius's Law.

For general storage conditions, then, an ambient temperature of about seventy degrees Fahrenheit is appropriate, with a relative humidity of 50 percent. A temperature lower than seventy degrees Fahrenheit is desirable, but it is more important to achieve environmental stability than it is to have low temperature conditions. Fluctuations should be kept to within plus or minus 10 percent of these values. When these conditions are maintained, most types of sound recordings will enjoy a long shelf life.

Monitoring of ambient conditions is an essential part of any preservation program. In situations where air conditioning already exists, it is important to determine whether it is functioning correctly. Often, it does not. Where there is no climate control, temperature and humidity data must be gathered to determine whether it is needed and, if so, to document that need. This requires the use of monitoring equipment.

Temperature- and humidity-monitoring equipment is available in a wide variety of types and prices. If a documentary record is needed for variations over a period of time, a chart or graph type of instrument is called for. These are expensive, ranging from three hundred to four hundred dollars up to the thousands. A good model is made by the Belfort Instrument Co., their Number 5–594. This device is spring powered and does not require any electricity. It can be positioned in any desired location. Chart recorders of that type must be calibrated before they are put into operation. That requires some care, although it is not difficult to do. The expense of purchasing this type of recorder can often be avoided by borrowing one from a local museum. Museum administrators and preservation or conservation officials are generally willing to make this kind of arrangement for other local, nonprofit organizations. This type of instrument is called a hygrothermograph.

Also available are smaller instruments that give temperature and relative humidity readings on a dial on a moment-to-moment basis, just as a thermometer does. These are generally priced from twenty dollars to one hundred dollars. Although convenient to use, they do not give a record of changes over a period of time and are not particularly accurate. A high-accuracy device for determining temperature and humidity is the psychrometer. The psychrometer registers relative humidity on being moistened and spun in the air. This is not a difficult procedure, and these items are low-priced, typically about twenty dollars. Here, as with the type of instruments with dials, if a documentary record is required, readings must be taken at regular intervals and recorded on a data sheet. Chart recorders as well as psychrometers and dial-type instruments are available from most scientific supply houses, such as Fisher and VWR. If there are problems in finding a supplier, a local museum can usually provide the necessary information.

For humidity monitoring only, an electronic, battery-powered instrument is available from Beckman Instruments, Incorporated. This device, called Humi-Chek II, provides relative humidity data on a moment-to-moment basis and has a reported accuracy of 2 percent. It comes with its own calibration standard and is priced at about $240.

While ambient temperature and humidity play the prime role in determining safe storage conditions for sound recordings, the question of the physical security of the storage environment should not be overlooked. It often seems that sound-recording collections, because they are used less intensively than other collections, are situated in out-of-the-way locations, in basements or on top floors. While basements offer the advantage of stable temperature, they are unsatisfactory in many respects, as are attics. Basements often, for example, have exposed utility conduits, such as water and steam pipes. The damage that a burst steam pipe can do to a collection of sound recordings is considerable. In addition, basement walls are sometimes subject to sweating or even leakage if original construction was not properly done. Finally, basements are particularly vulnerable to flooding as a result of external events. Attics and other top-floor locations often become hot in summer months or when heating is not controlled. For that reason, and because of the danger of leakage, they do not make a good location for a sound archives.

The above factors should be seriously analyzed when the question of storage location arises. While at least three major sound archives in this country are located in basements and have so far avoided disaster, these locations are far from ideal. As a general principle, no archival collection should be located near utility conduits, elevator shafts, roofs, or basements or other situations where flooding, fire, or smoke damage would be maximized. Along with good location, any collection of sound recordings of appreciable value should have emergency monitoring facilities, such as remote-temperature or smoke sensors, as well as fire and flood prevention-and-control equipment and adequate protection against theft.

There is disagreement among preservation experts on the best methods of fire control. Advocates fall into two groups: wet (sprinkler) and dry methods. Both approaches effectively control fire. Sprinklers, unfortunately, do it in a way that can cause as much damage to archival materials as fire or smoke itself. At least three sound archives in this country have sprinkler methods of fire control. These include the Library of Congress, Rodgers and Hammerstein, and Yale University. Dry methods of control usually employ gas to extinguish fires. A sensor detects either high temperatures or smoke, which in turn causes a valve to release large quantities of gas into the atmosphere. The gas interferes with the fire, either by depriving it of oxygen or heat. Different types of gasses are used, including carbon dioxide and certain organohalogens. These are nontoxic. Gas systems have several advantages. First, once the fire has been extinguished, the atmosphere need only be cleared of the control agents. There is no destruction, other than that caused by the fire itself. Second, gas systems can be installed in individual rooms—they do not necessarily require central equipment, as do sprinklers. That is a big advantage where cost is a concern. On the other hand, gas systems have disadvantages. Gas cylinders must be periodically recharged to maintain pressure. Furthermore, where there is a fire and a gas system is discharging, oxygen levels in a sealed room can reach low levels, posing a threat to any people who might happen to be trapped in the room. On the whole, gas systems seem to offer greater convenience than sprinklers and will probably be chosen in more and more archives.

Although a number of sound archives are located in basements, none seems to have given serious consideration to flooding emergencies. An exception is the German National Radio Archives in Hamburg. There, a system of floor baffles was installed to control the movement of water. Pumps are provided to remove water quickly from the basement before it reaches the lowest stack levels.[1]

A simple way to keep damage from flooding to a minimum in basement locations is not to shelve any items at floor level. Shelving can begin, for example, at three to four feet above the floor. While that offers protection against minor flooding, it would probably not be of much use in the event of a major catastrophe and is achieved only at the expense of considerable shelving space, almost always at a premium. A far better approach is not to locate any archive in a basement.

Emergency equipment cannot be depended on to operate in a disaster unless it is periodically inspected and tested. The archivist or librarian should not leave that task to the building maintenance staff. A personal interest is necessary, to ensure that inspections are regularly performed and to familiarize oneself with the equipment and the way it is supposed to function.

Several other general storage conditions should be mentioned. Particularly relevant to storage of sound recordings is the problem of dust level. It has already been stated that sound recordings are elements designed to fit into a mechanical playback system. Because sound information is contained in minute physical units, such as disc grooves or magnetic tape domaines, the interposition of any small-diameter foreign matter into these spaces will create

1. Dietrich Lotichius, "Safety First—Essential in the Preservation of Sound Recordings," *Phonographic Bulletin* 5 (December 1972): 8–14.

distortion in the playback process. It is therefore advantageous to keep dust levels in sound-recording storage areas as low as possible. The ideal situation is a positive-pressure storage area in which air conditioning keeps the air pressure within the storage area higher than that in adjacent rooms. That way, dust cannot enter. In such an arrangement—common in record mastering studios and tape-storage areas for computers—the air entering the storage area is carefully filtered to remove dust. This is an expensive arrangement to build and maintain, and most sound archives cannot afford it.

A less expensive method of dust control, although one that is by no means cheap, is to store sound recordings in well-constructed wooden or steel cabinets with tight-fitting doors. The use of cabinets isolates the sound recordings, to a considerable degree, from dust and other airborne contaminants, thereby providing an excellent storage environment. Cabinets suitable for housing sound recordings will, in most instances, have to be specially ordered, depending on the kind of items in the collection, the size of the collection, and the dimensions of storage rooms. (Most library supply companies market cabinets suitable for archival storage of cassettes and seven-inch reel-to-reel tapes, but the kinds of cabinets they offer for discs are generally not adequate.) For a good-sized collection, the cost of special cabinets will run into tens of thousands of dollars. For a small collection, on the other hand, the cost would not be great, and the use of cabinets becomes a practical way to provide a good storage environment. For a very large collection, cabinets would almost surely be out of the question.

Whether open shelving or cabinets are employed, a regular cleaning and vacuuming program is essential. Frequency of vacuuming must be determined by the rate at which dust accumulates. That, in turn, will be affected by the general environment of the archive (urban, suburban, rural) and whether the building in which an archive is located has central air conditioning. Central air conditioning systems almost always have dust filters that reduce the amount of incoming dust to individual rooms. This is of significant value in the control process.

Visible light and ultraviolet radiation (from fluorescent lighting fixtures), serious problems in storing printed materials, are not destructive to record and tape collections, provided elevated temperatures are not generated. Recorded materials are shielded from light by packaging. The packaging itself, in some instances interesting in its own right, may fade or yellow, in time, if exposed to ultraviolet radiation. Ultraviolet filters may be obtained for fluorescent lights, the main indoor source of ultraviolet radiation. The Library of Congress maintains its sound-recording stacks in darkness when they are not being used. Other archives are illuminated during working hours.

Sound recordings have been produced in many formats and materials, each having specific storage requirements. These will be developed for each main class of sound recording.

Storage Requirements for Discs

While discs require good environmental conditions for effective preservation, of great importance to their well-being is correct physical positioning. The disc shape is a vulnerable one and is particularly sensitive to improper loading. This vulnerability means that the disc can easily be deformed if subject to external physical stress.

Probably the ideal way to store a disc would be to lay it by itself on a perfectly flat shelf, which would support it equally at all points on one side. That would be impractical, however, because, in a collection of any size, the shelving would occupy more space than the discs. As a consequence, the only realistic way to store discs is immediately next to each other.

Horizontal stacking in most situations is not advisable because the weight of the discs combines to create significant stress on the discs lowest in the stack. The most practical and safe way of storing discs is on end in a vertical arrangement. That method is used in the overwhelming majority of situations. Although it has some disadvantages, they are exceeded by its benefits.

When vertical disc storage is used, the discs—either in original packaging or in special envelopes—are arranged on horizontal shelves, usually of the familiar adjustable metal library type. Heavy-duty shelving is ordinarily required for disc storage because the accumulated weight of four or five hundred discs, whether shellac or vinyl, is considerable. The shelving should be wide enough to accommodate the discs of widest diameter to be

Fig. 1. Multiple-disc sets stored vertically on heavy-duty metal library shelving. Due to their width, boxed sets tend to remain vertical without the need for subdivisions. Dividers should be provided, nonetheless. In an archives, identification labels should not be attached to original packaging, as they are in the illustration. Items may be identified by manufacturers' serial numbers or by inserted flags.

stored. It is not safe to permit discs to protrude beyond shelf width. They can be easily damaged that way. In some archives, fixed wooden shelving has been used, but unless it has already been installed, that kind of shelving is usually very expensive and does not offer the flexibility of adjustable metal shelving.

The main problem that can arise in vertical arrangement of discs is slanting loads. It is important that discs stored vertically be *fully vertical at all times*. Discs should not be tilting at an angle against each other. Discs packaged and stored in sufficiently large boxed sets will not tilt, but such sets generally do not predominate in archival collections. For most discs, including 78s and LPs, slanting is a serious problem. Slanting loads cause warpage. That, in turn, has an adverse effect on playback capability and therefore on sonic content. Although warping can be corrected, in some instances, it is at best a time-consuming procedure. For many

Fig. 2. Individual long-playing discs in vertical storage with metal sub-dividers. Note that the discs do not protrude beyond the shelving. Special packaging may be provided for discs where intensive use would damage dust jackets, as in a music library. In an archives, this would be neither necessary nor desirable.

discs, warping *cannot* be corrected, and the damage will be permanent.

The solution most often used to avoid slanting is to divide each shelf into vertical compartments or subdivisions. This is accomplished by the inclusion of fixed spacing panels so that no more than about twenty discs are stored in each vertical subdivision. Typically, this means that the dividers will be spaced about 3½ inches to 4 inches apart. That allows the discs to be loosely shelved next to each other and yet remain vertical, even when one or two are removed for auditioning. Each division should be fully filled with discs under normal circumstances. When there are insufficient discs to fill a space, a book or other object can be inserted in the division to ensure that the discs will remain vertical.

An ingenious solution to providing vertical subdivisions has been found by the Library of Congress in housing its large collection of LPs. Cardboard containers are provided that are wide enough to accommodate about twenty twelve-inch LPs in original packaging. One end of the container is permanently open (it has no side). The discs are vertically filed in the container with the spines on the open side, allowing serial numbers and titles to be visible. The containers are then placed on the metal shelving in rows. This arrangement has several advantages. First, it is a convenient and economical way to provide vertical subdivisions on standard library shelves. Second, it will effectively keep the discs upright. Third, it is a considerable help when shifting of items becomes necessary. Discs can be easily moved in groups using the containers. Other large sound archives have wooden shelving with permanently installed wooden or masonite dividers. The use of book ends to provide vertical subdivisions is not recommended. Book ends will not fully accomplish their purpose and can cause warping.

Most archives and music libraries will elect to arrange discs by size. Appropriate shelving and dividers would then be provided for each size of disc. Where a small number of 45s is to be accommodated, horizontal arrangement is possible. It has been suggested by one sound archivist that these seven-inch discs be stored in original packaging, horizontally, in small trays.[2] Because 45s are much lighter in weight than 78s, this is a possible way of dealing with them. The discs at the bottom of a small stack would not be seriously stressed. This method would not be practical for a large collection.

One theoretical disadvantage to vertical arrangement of discs is gravity loading. When discs are stored vertically, the entire weight of the disc is concentrated on one point on its circumference. The kind of plastic materials of which discs are made, including polystyrene, vinyl, and shellac, are subject to a very slow type of flowing—the material is not absolutely fixed in shape. Over a long period of time, it is conceivable that a disc would become thicker and gradually spread out at the point where the weight was concentrated. This problem has been investigated. The conclusion of the researchers was that gravity loading was not an important consideration within a time span of a hundred years.[3] If

2. Walter L. Welch, "Preservation and Restoration of Authenticity in Sound Recordings," *Library Trends* 21 (July 1972): 95.

3. A. G. Pickett and M. M. Lemcoe, *Preservation and Storage of Sound Recordings* (Washington: Library of Congress, 1959), pp. 41–42.

it is planned to retain discs for great periods of time, they can be rotated a quarter-turn every five or ten years to ensure that whatever gravity loading effects might be occurring are evened out.

Environmental Conditions

Discs will do well in the ambient conditions outlined for general storage requirements—seventy degrees F. and 50 percent R.H., with as much absence of cycling as possible. Temperatures lower than seventy degrees F. are desirable but are usually expensive to maintain in areas with warm, humid summers. Lower temperatures will have little effect on the shelf life of the discs themselves—rather, it is the paper products in which the discs are packaged that benefit from it. Temperatures below thirty-two degrees F. are not recommended. Shellac and vinyl will become brittle below zero degrees F. Temperatures much higher than seventy degrees F. should be avoided if at all possible. In no case should temperatures exceed eighty degrees F.

The Library of Congress maintains record stacks at seventy-two degrees F. year-round. Relative humidity in the library's record stacks is allowed to vary seasonally. Because Washington, D.C., has unusually humid summers, it is not economically feasible to maintain exact control over humidity. That is likely to be true in many areas of the southeastern United States. While every effort should be made to minimize hygroscopic cycling (changes in humidity) this is less important for discs than it is for other sound-recording media, such as tapes, and seasonal variation is acceptable. A problem in northern states is low winter humidity, but that is not expensive to correct, with the use of humidifiers.

Packaging

Packaging of discs has a direct bearing on the success with which they are preserved. In many instances, original packaging is adequate, while in others it will have a detrimental effect on disc life. Packaging considerations are determined by these factors and also by institutional budget. Disc packaging can be expensive.

Modern LPs normally come from the manufacturer packaged in a clear cellophane shrink-wrapper, as protection for the dust jacket; next, they are put in a paper box or dust jacket, to provide some rigidity and over-all protection for the disc; and finally, they are encased in an inner liner, made of either polyethylene, glassine, or paper, for protection of the disc grooves. Given proper shelving and ambient conditions, that type of packaging is adequate for long-term storage, with one important exception. The outer cellophane shrink-wrapping should *always* be removed from any disc as soon after it has been acquired as possible. Shrink-wrapping is highly temperature-sensitive and can contract, causing disc warpage.

Many archives and libraries store LPs in original packaging. Ideally, however, paper or glassine inner linings should not be retained. Both paper and glassine, unless specially treated, contain acid that can migrate to the disc and attack the vinyl surfaces. Paper is also a hospitable environment for fungi. Some sound archives, such as the Collection of Historical Sound Recordings at Yale University, routinely package all LPs in polyethylene inner liners. That policy is recommended. Polyethylene liners are available from standard library-supply houses.

Shellac 78s present different problems, and it is generally not a good idea to store them in original packaging (it may, however, be desirable to retain original packaging, separately, for historical purposes). Many 78s were issued in sets consisting of albums with bound-in paper envelopes for the discs. These are not safe for 78s because of the tendency of the bound envelopes to break the discs. Most sound archives store 78s, whether they be single discs or parts of sets, in individual paper envelopes.

The Library of Congress, through its funding of the Pickett-Lemcoe study of 1959, pioneered in the development of packaging for 78s. The library currently stores all nonrare 78s in liners made to specifications drawn up by Robert Carneal, Chief Engineer of its Recorded-Sound Section. These liners are of thirty-five-pound kraft paper and are manufactured by the Hollinger Corporation, a well-known supplier of archival products. They are of acid-free paper and offer excellent storage for 78s with a minimum of interaction between disc and paper.

The Hollinger Corporation, which originally supplied record jackets in large orders only, has now developed a product comparable to the Library of Congress packaging that can be ordered in smaller lots. The product consists of a record jacket of kraft paper exterior and foil liner. The jacket can be heat-sealed on top to encapsulate the disc for long-term storage and is available in lots of one hundred in twelve-inch and sixteen-inch sizes. Recently, a new firm has entered the market, the Process Materials Corporation. They are manufacturing plain (un-lined) disc jackets of acid-free paper in ten-inch and twelve-inch sizes. They will be supplying this product to Yale and to Rodgers and Hammerstein. These jackets have holes for viewing disc labels and hence cannot be sealed.

For particularly rare 78s, the Library of Congress uses a modified version of the elaborate package designed for them by Pickett and Lemcoe. This involves a paper sleeve for the record itself, which, in turn, is sealed in a transparent plastic envelope. A picture of the record and a close-up of the labels on both sides is sealed inside the plastic, visible from the outside. The technique isolates the disc from dust and changes in humidity. It is used only for records that have been taped. The entire Secrist Collection of early operatic recordings is housed in these envelopes.

Acetate and nitrate discs are also best stored in paper envelopes. In fact, they should never be placed in polyethylene liners. Under certain conditions of temperature and humidity, the plastic will bond with the acetate or nitrate. When the disc is removed from the jacket, the acetate or nitrate, adhering to the liner, will be pulled off its aluminum or glass backing and the recording destroyed.

Disc Washing

The need for maintaining a clean, low-dust environment for sound recordings has already been stated. It is important that the sound recordings themselves also be kept clean. Cleaning of discs can take place at two different stages: before, during, and after playback and before the discs are put into storage. Cleaning in relation to playback will be discussed in the section on use. This involves the cleaning of individual discs. Cleaning prior to storage will generally mean processing of discs in large quantities. It is most often employed when new materials are entering the library or archives, materials that have, in all likelihood, been stored in less than ideal circumstances, or when it is desired to process materials already on hand that may never have been cleaned.

The advisability of cleaning prior to storage is apparent. Foreign matter resting on or in the grooves of discs can only have an adverse effect on discs that may be unused from year to year. Such foreign matter can include dust, mold, and particles of paper or other packing material. It is not uncommon, when opening a crate of acetates, for example, to find the records covered with a combination of castor oil (which has separated from the acetate and oozed to the surface), excelsior, wood chips, and cardboard shreds. Dirty conditions such as that will encourage the growth of fungi and mold and contribute to deterioration originating in the discs themselves.

A number of cleaning methods are available for different types of discs. All involve washing. While washing can improve the condition of records, it can also harm them if it is not done correctly or if the wrong kinds of discs are washed. For that reason, washing should not be attempted unless there appears to be a serious need for it—that is, unless discs are covered with visible dirt or debris. Certain types of discs—laminated shellacs, which include most Columbia 78s, and all instantaneous recordings—should not be exposed to water. If a washing program is decided upon, discs must be screened to eliminate those that cannot tolerate moisture. In addition, it is wise to experiment with washing techniques on expendable records before washing a collection's rarer items.

The basic requirements for washing include a clean, shallow, plastic basin large enough to accommodate the largest discs to be washed; distilled water; liquid detergent (Joy is good); soft cotton chamois cloths; and a rack to hold records vertically while they are drying.

A washing solution should be prepared consisting of luke-warm distilled water and detergent. Different authorities have recommended different concentrations of detergent. One teaspoon per gallon is a concentrated solution useful for cleaning dirty records. The minimum concentration recommended is sixteen drops per gallon. Kodak Fotoflo 200 may be used in place of detergent, since the principal purpose of the detergent is to prevent the formation of drops during the drying process. It is important to use distilled water. Tap water contains dissolved minerals that can precipitate in crystalline form in record grooves during drying. That will create noise and distortion.

Each disc is immersed in the solution, and the surfaces are gently rubbed with a soft cloth for about thirty seconds. The

Fig. 3. In some instances, disc washing may improve playback quality. This is particularly true for discs that have accumulated visible amounts of dust, debris, and so on. Discs are immersed in a solution of water and detergent or Kodak Fotoflo. The detergent acts to dissolve grease and to reduce the formation of drops during the drying process. Discs are rubbed with a soft cotton cloth and set on racks to dry. A 14-by-17-inch photographic developing tray makes a convenient washing basin.

grooves should be cleaned on both sides of the disc, using a circular motion, rubbing in the direction of the grooves and not across them. When washing is completed, the disc is removed from the water and wiped with a soft, lint-free cloth to remove excess water. The discs are then placed in a rack to dry. Rinsing is unnecessary, so long as the washing solution does not become dirty (the washing solution should be changed frequently if large numbers of discs are being processed). The Watts Company makes a brush for washing records. It is a useful product, quite inexpensive, and may be used in place of a soft cotton cloth.

Drying is perhaps the most crucial stage in the washing process. It is during drying that dust can settle on the disc surface and stick there due to the surface tension of the water. Discs should therefore be dried in a low-dust environment. Compressed air can be used to dry discs if it does not have a high aerosol content (that is, it should be free from impurities such as oil vapor, and so on). During washing, record labels will sometimes come off. These should be saved and pressed dry between sheets of heavy blotting paper on top of which a weight has been placed. The weight helps to prevent them from wrinkling during drying. They can later be reattached to the discs.

Even by using these hand-washing methods, a surprisingly large number of discs can be processed. The Milwaukee Public Library recently washed some 27,000 78s during a six-month period. The average rate was 70 to 80 discs per hour.[4] Volunteers can sometimes be recruited for this kind of activity. There is a widespread interest in sound recordings, particularly among younger people.

Libraries or archives with large collections of shellac 78s will be interested in the washing technique developed at the Library of Congress. There, shellac discs are gripped between round rubber holders (which keep water off the record labels) and lowered into a water-and-detergent solution. Ultrasonic energy at twenty, thirty, and fifty kHz causes dirt and other foreign matter to vibrate loose from disc grooves. After a twenty-second period, the discs are removed and dried with compressed air or a soft cotton chamois cloth.

Instantaneous recordings, often stored in poor conditions, present washing problems. Because the residue on acetates and nitrates is often oil-based, or contaminated with oil, water is ineffective in cleaning them. An organic solvent, that will degrease the records and at the same time have a minimal effect on acetate and nitrate coatings is necessary. Such a solvent is Freon TF, a nontoxic organohalogen, available from most technical supply houses or from a local Dupont distributor. Instantaneous recordings can be degreased in Freon TF in a manner similar to that used for washing shellacs. Unfortunately, because of the soft surfaces of acetates, it is dangerous to rub them directly. Simple immersion, however, will dissolve much of the grease. Other material can be removed from them by very light wiping with a cotton chamois.

4. Peter A. Grendysa, "Taking Care of 78s," *Record Exchanger* 4, no. 1 (n.d.): 19.

Acetates should be set on a rack to dry—compressed air or manual wiping will damage the delicate surfaces. Because Freon TF has a very low boiling point, cleaning records with it should take place in as cold a room as possible. Otherwise, there will be considerable loss of the Freon through evaporation. The same basins and other equipment used to process acetates should not be used for shellacs or LPs.

The Library of Congress uses an ultrasonic bath of Freon TF for cleaning acetates. In their set-up, a zone of refrigerated air directly above the bath causes excess Freon on the disc to be condensed as the discs are removed. The discs are handled by the same rubber grip used for shellacs. Ultrasonic vibration is the preferred method of cleaning acetates.

All vinyl discs may be washed without damage to the vinyl itself. The procedure for washing them is the same as for washing shellacs. Freon TF may be used on vinyl discs if desired. Here, as with shellacs, washing should only be carried out if the discs are really dirty (dirt is visible to the naked eye). Separate equipment should be kept for washing vinyl and shellac discs. Grit from shellac can damage vinyl surfaces.

While washing is a good way of removing gross accumulations of foreign matter from discs, it is not usually effective in removing microscopic dirt lying in groove bottoms and cannot be expected to solve such problems as crackle or other forms of disc noise. Crackle, ticks, and pops, once they have developed, are generally permanent, and the only way to remove them is through electronic processing. In some instances, washing discs may even make this problem worse. It should be pointed out that not all experts agree on the advisability of washing. Percy Wilson, a much-respected British audio engineer, has warned against it unless suction drying is used.[5] On the other hand, Cecil Watts, known for the Watts Dust Bug, has recommended washing of LPs in cases where particle build-up on groove walls has become substantial.[6]

Where washing cannot be employed to clean discs, the methods of dry-cleaning described in the section on use may be substituted.

5. Percy Wilson, "Care of Records," *Audio* 56 (December 1972): 32.
6. "Just for the Record; an Invaluable Guide for Helping You Protect, Maintain and Preserve Your Records" (New Hyde Park, N.Y.: Elpa Marketing Industries, 1975), pp. 24–25.

An effective, although expensive, machine for washing discs is the Keith Monks record-washer. In this system, priced at about $1,800, a vacuum removes water and suspended dust from the disc surface as the disc is washed. This prevents dust from being redeposited or trapped in the groove walls during the drying process, one of the principal drawbacks of disc-washing. The machine is safe for records and works quite well. Its price would preclude its application in all but the largest collections.

When any item is in long-term storage, the question of that item's inherent stability should be examined. Many materials are not inherently stable—they possess what preservation experts refer to as "inherent vice." Materials subject to inherent vice will gradually self-destruct if left untreated. Almost all printed materials produced after 1850 fall into this category, including almost all present-day printing, little of which can be expected to last more than a hundred years. Most sound recordings are free from inherent vice.

Properly formulated shellac will "cure" as it ages. The "curing" involves a cross-linking phenomenon between the polymerized molecules, similar to the bonding that takes place between adjacent fibers of cellulose. Cured shellac deforms less readily than new, is more elastic, and appears to be relatively free of oxidation-reduction reactions that produce acid in other kinds of archival and library materials. Cheaper grades of shellac, typically those produced during World Wars I and II, will not be as structurally stable as cured shellac. However, there is no evidence that deleterious chemical reactions are taking place within these discs.

The chemistry of vinyl discs is different. Hydrochloric acid is slowly produced in the disc over a period of years as a result of oxidation-reduction reactions. If vinyl were not treated, it would gradually deteriorate. Fortunately, the problem of hydrochloric acid formation also occurs in the manufacturing process. Acid formation is significant at the temperatures at which discs are molded. To control that problem, manufacturers add to the vinyl compound a chemical stabilizer that absorbs the acid. Enough of this stabilizer remains after manufacture to continue to protect the disc, absorbing the minute quantities of acid produced for many years. Most LPs are therefore free from inherent vice. Improperly formulated LPs, especially those with inadequate stabilizer, will deteriorate, and nothing can be done to prevent that. The deterioration will show up only after many years on the shelf.

Pickett and Lemcoe reached the following conclusions on the long-term outlook for vinyl discs:

1. They will remain chemically stable as long as stabilizers are present.

2. There will be little warp due to gravity loads if they are kept vertical and at temperatures below 80°F.

3. Serious warp will occur as a result of thermal cycling. Storage temperatures should be kept stable. Warp due to the relaxation of inner microscopic stresses is inhibited at temperatures below 70°F.

4. Humidity control is not essential.[7]

The situation in regard to 45s is less satisfactory. Early 45s were made from vinyl or a vinyl-and-shellac combination that is stable. It was soon discovered, however, that polystyrene could be used to make 45s in an injection-molding technique that offered cost savings. Many 45s were made from polystyrene, and still are. An aura of commercialism has always surrounded 45s, with records being issued by companies whose last concern has been disc quality. It has now been established that polystyrene discs are inherently unstable. Internal stresses can cause the discs to fracture from the 1½-inch center hole outward. Unfortunately, no research has been done in this field. There does not appear, however, to be anything that can be done to retard or prevent this process. One of the strongest areas of collector interest at this time is centered around 45s. The preservation of 45s is an important area for future study.

Instantaneous recordings—those made on a cellulose acetate or nitrate base—pose the single most serious problem for sound archivists. These records, produced in large quantities in the 1930s and '40s, will often form a significant part of a sound archive's or library's holdings. They are unstable from almost every point of view. First, the cellulose compounds decompose due to oxidation-reduction reactions in which acetic or nitric acid is formed. The discs become brittle and eventually crumble. Second, bonding

7. Pickett, *Preservation*, pp. 41–42.

between the recording medium and the backing of the disc tends to break down, with the result that the coating peels or flakes away, along with the recorded sound. Third, castor oil was usually added to the acetate or nitrate, both as a plasticizer (to make it more receptive to the cutting head) and to improve its adherence to the base. In time, the castor oil will separate from the acetate, rising to the surface of the record and producing a greasy film. This renders the record unplayable.

Because of the grave inherent instability of instantaneous recordings, most sound archives seek to tape them as soon as possible. This is the only realistic way to preserve sonic content. Not much hope can be put in preserving instantaneous recordings as physical objects. The best that can be done in that respect is to provide excellent storage conditions, with acid-free paper envelopes. Most instantaneous records should be cleaned prior to being put in storage.

Storage Requirements for Tape

Modern reel-to-reel magnetic tape on 1.5-mil mylar backing is perhaps the best all-around storage vehicle for recorded sound. It is free of inherent vice, and there is little that can be done to damage it, short of gross abuse. To take full advantage of its potential, however, it must be stored under proper conditions. When that is done, it will last indefinitely. Reels of tape have been included in time capsules.

Tape, whether in reel-to-reel or cassette format, is handled and stored on reels of various sizes. In order for tape to move onto and off reels smoothly and to be wound evenly, it is kept under tension by the tape machine. That means that the tape is wound under tension and stored on the reel under tension. Modern tape is designed to sustain normal playback or recording tension without deformation. When that tension is exceeded, however, deformation will occur, resulting in distortion or loss of sonic content. Tape can also be damaged by insufficient tension. For these reasons, correct winding tension is an essential aspect of tape storage and use.

Tape tension is primarily determined by the tape machine. Tension varies at different stages of the operation cycle. During playback and record mode, when the tape is moving at a standard speed, tension is low, between two and three ounces for a quarter-inch tape, and it remains relatively constant. In rewind and fast-forward modes, however, tension fluctuates and is generally higher than in playback mode. It is for this reason that any tape that is going into storage should be wound on the storage reel at playback speed, not at fast-forward or rewind speed. In other words, tapes should be stored "played," not "rewound." This form of storage is referred to as "tails out," because the end of the tape, after it has been played through, will be on the outside of the reel.

Tape machines in a good state of repair will generally maintain appropriate tension during playback mode. That can be checked by visual inspection of the wound reel. The tape should be evenly wound, producing a flat surface with no ridges or creases. Ridges frequently result from winding at fast-forward or rewind speeds. Ridges are a good indication that tension is too high when tape has been wound at playback speed. Low tension is revealed by cinching, where the tape buckles or slips back over itself. Cinching is not a common problem with quarter-inch audio tapes. It will be encountered more often in two-inch audio and video tapes. When improper tape tensioning is suspected, the tape machine will require adjustment. Some tape decks provide instructions for adjusting winding tension. This is true of fully professional tape decks. Most "audiophile" classes of tape decks do not provide instructions, because the necessary adjustments must be made inside the machine. Thus, anyone working with that type of tape deck will probably be forced to call in a service technician to check and adjust winding tension. It is possible for the technically inclined to obtain service manuals from the manufacturer or distributor and adjust tape tension themselves.

As a practical matter, tails-out storage has one disadvantage. In order to wind the tape at low tension, it must be fully played through, which may take anywhere from fifteen minutes to two or more hours. In a situation where use of a recorded-sound collection is minimal, and some regular staffing is available, that will present no difficulties. Where there is sustained use, however, the problem of finding staff and time to wind the tapes is serious. Usually, it is only possible to adhere to a strict "tails-out" policy at institutions with large staffs. For example, the Library of Congress maintains a uniform compliance with its tails-out policy. Other large sound archives with smaller staffs, while they have a tails-out policy, cannot maintain it at all times. In theory, it is important to do so.

It is sometimes suggested that, to relieve tension built up in tapes held in long-term storage, tapes be played through every six to twelve months. There is no documentary evidence to back that claim, and no major sound archives has such a policy. The Minnesota Mining and Manufacturing Company (3M) has stated that this procedure is unnecessary for good-quality modern tapes, but that it may be advisable for older tapes.[8] That would include tapes on an acetate base (although acetate-base tapes should be dubbed onto mylar base at the earliest opportunity, since acetate is inherently unstable).

Environmental Conditions

Tape, regardless of its formulation, is sensitive to variations in temperature and humidity. Although that sensitivity on a unit-length basis is not so great as that of some other sound-recording materials, it can result in the creation of enormous stresses due to tape length. Up to half a mile of 1.5-mil tape may be contained on a standard 10½-inch reel. Small shrinkages or expansions, when amplified by the total length of the tape, become large.

The creation of changing stresses in tape by thermal and hygroscopic cycling will result in the gradual deterioration of sonic content. In its most severe form, it will result in changes in pitch and timing and/or in print-through, the transfer of sonic information from one band of tape to its neighbor, resulting in an audible double-sound image, as well as loss of the oxide coating. More subtle forms of deterioration include distortion and tape drop-out (drop-out represents a minute break in the continuity of recorded information).

Tape should therefore be stored under conditions of very little thermal or hygroscopic cycling. Ambient conditions in the storage environment are more critical for tapes than for discs. A temperature variation of not greater than plus or minus five degrees F. and no more than plus or minus 10 percent relative humidity variation is best for tapes.

8. "Retentivity" (St. Paul, Minn.: 3M Company, Magnetic Audio/Visual Products Division, n.d.), p. 4.

The Library of Congress keeps its tapes in a special, individually air-conditioned storage area enclosed in sheet metal. The air conditioning employed is in addition to the building air conditioning. The purpose of the extra system is to keep cycling at an absolute minimum. A low temperature is maintained at all times, while relative humidity is kept between 30 to 50 percent in the winter and 45 to 50 percent in summer.

A low absolute temperature should be maintained for tapes, provided that it can be consistently regulated. Low absolute temperatures minimize print-through and the development of fungi. Temperatures in tape-storage areas should not exceed seventy degrees F. A better temperature for tapes is sixty degrees F. In almost every situation, that will require a special air-conditioning arrangement. Aside from the few extremely large sound archives in this country, most tape collections will not exceed the size of one or two rooms. Stable conditions in these areas can be achieved using proper insulation and room air conditioners. An air-conditioning specialist can determine the correct rating of room units, based on the physical situation of the archive and the type of climate of the geographical location.

By the same token, a low relative humidity should also be maintained, mainly to protect the tape from fungus growth. Although fungus is not so serious a problem with tape as it is with discs, it can occur, particularly on tapes that have been spliced. Growth takes place at the splicing site. A figure of between 40 percent and 50 percent relative humidity is adequate for tapes.

If tapes are to be transferred from an air-conditioned storage area to a non-air-conditioned use area, they should be given twenty-four hours to acclimate to the new environment before being placed on tape machines. Ideally, of course, use areas should also to be air conditioned.

Accidental Erasure

Because a magnetic field is used to create a tape recording (by magnetizing the iron-oxide coating on the tape), a magnetic field can also change or erase a recording. Tapes can be deliberately erased on a tape machine through a high-frequency alternating current acting through a magnetic head. Tapes can also be erased, however, by external magnetic fields. A bulk eraser is such a device. It can be used to erase an entire tape in a few seconds.

Accidental exposure to magnetic fields can also erase tapes, and this is a matter of some concern where long-term storage of tapes is involved.

A magnetic field is generated whenever electricity passes through a wire. Particularly strong magnetic fields are generated when current passes through coiled wire or when very great currents pass through straight wire. All electrical motors have coiled wire inside, which produces magnetic fields—as do electronic and radio equipment and electrical conduits. Thus, stray magnetic fields are not uncommon, and fear is often expressed for the safety of magnetic tapes.

In practice, accidental erasure from external magnetic fields is a problem that almost never arises. Electromagnetic energy emanating from a single source dissipates in geometric proportion to the distance from that source. Magnetic energy is measured in oersteds. A source of 1,500 oersteds, which constitutes a powerful magnetic field, has an effective energy of only 50 oersteds at a distance of 2.7 inches. It has been determined that a magnetic energy of 50 oersteds immediately adjacent to a tape recording has no audible effect on the tape.[9] If tapes are kept at least three inches away from electrical conduits, electric motors, or other sources of magnetic energy, there should be no danger of accidental erasure. As a general principal, of course, tapes should not be located any nearer to possible sources of magnetic energy than necessary. The only sources of serious trouble likely to be encountered in an archive or library would be location of the storage area next to high-voltage lines or transformers. That should be avoided, even though the possibility of erasure from these sources is not great, so long as immediate contact does not occur.

There is no evidence to suggest that placing tapes on metal shelves in any way affects the tapes. Many sound archives have stored tapes on metal shelving for years with no loss of sound quality. There are some archivists, however, who do not recommend placing magnetic tapes on metal shelves, preferring the use of wooden shelving for this purpose.

Dust and Packaging
Tape-storage areas should be kept free of dust. Dust can con-

9. "Retentivity," p. 2.

tribute to drop-out if it becomes trapped between layers of tape. Dust and grit entering the layers of tape can also damage the backing and the magnetic coating. In professional and scientific situations, tapes are usually recorded, stored, and played in a "clean-room" environment, where there is positive pressure and air filtration. Since most archives or libraries cannot afford that, a regular cleaning-and-dusting program must be established. That fact is emphasized in most literature on tape storage.

A good way to help reduce the dust problem is to keep tape reels inside polyethylene bags. These are normally supplied with new tape and should be retained for this purpose. Additional bags can be obtained for tapes that do not have them; "Baggies" sandwich bags are acceptable. The bags can be sealed with Scotch tape, or the open edges can be folded over to make a seal. Polyethylene bags not only prevent dust from getting onto the tape, they also tend to reduce the effects of thermal and hygroscopic cycling, particularly the latter. The use of cabinets for tape storage will also help.

Tapes are supplied new in individual boxes. They should be shelved in them, as the boxes provide good protection for the reel, as well as additional dust protection. Boxes also permit convenient and safe handling of tapes. As with discs, boxes of tapes should be kept vertical on the shelf. If they are not, distortions in reel shape can develop—particularly with plastic reels—which will ultimately cause the tape to wind unevenly. Boxes make useful filing units and can be arranged by box size, which is more or less standardized. Boxes should be provided for any tapes that do not have them.

Properly manufactured 1.5-mil mylar-base magnetic tape has little, if any, inherent vice. Its long-term stability in proper storage conditions is excellent. Manufacturing standards, however, are not always consistent. When tape is not processed correctly, a residual of chloride may remain, which, through oxidation-reduction reactions, can be converted into hydrochloric acid.

Many tapes in an archival collection will have been donated or made at a time when it was not possible to check tape quality. When that is the case, the archivist has no control over what kind of tape goes into storage. Many archives, however, have an active taping program for which it is possible to select a good-quality

Fig. 4. Reel-to-reel tapes stored vertically in original boxes. Standard metal library shelving is employed. There is no evidence suggesting that metal shelves affect the sound quality of magnetic tapes.

tape. Either way, it is advisable to test tapes, to determine whether they should be dubbed onto better tape or to detect manufacturing defects.

A simple test to determine the chlorine content of a tape is to burn a piece of it. If it produces a green flame, chlorine is present, and the tape is unsuitable for long-term storage. If tape is purchased in large quantities, it is possible to ask manufacturers or distributors to submit samples, which can be tested for chlorine content prior to ordering. Another way to test tape is to scratch the magnetic coating with any pointed instrument, such as a nail file. It will be possible to determine which tape, among different samples, has the strongest adherence between backing and coating.

Tape other than 1.5-mil mylar should be avoided for long-term storage. Although mylar has been used as a backing for many years, not all mylar tapes will occur in the 1.5-mil thickness. Many, if not most, amateur tapes will be found on 1.0- or .5-mil tape. These thinner tapes have a number of undesirable qualities. They are prone to stretching and other forms of dimensional distortion; they tear and break more easily than 1.5-mil; and print-through is greater. The reason they are often employed in amateur recording is that more tape can be contained on the same reel, and hence more recording time is available. Mylar in less than 1.5-mil thickness is chemically as stable as the thicker mylar, but should be rejected as a storage vehicle.

Cellulose acetate-base tapes, the first kind to come into commercial use in this country, are inherently unstable, just as are their disc counterparts. With age they will become brittle and eventually decompose. They have other undesirable properties, including high thermal and hygroscopic co-efficiencies of expansion, low wind stability and low tensile strength.[10] It is standard practice to retape important material contained on these tapes.

Few archives will have material on paper-base tape. Paper-base tape cannot be expected to have good long-term storage characteristics. Such tapes should be dubbed to mylar at the earliest opportunity. Care should be exercised in dubbing paper or very old acetate tape. Processing through some tape machines can cause severe damage to brittle tapes. In the opinion of some archivists, 3M tape decks offer smoothest handling for deteriorating tapes.

Cassettes

The principal tape format collected and stored by sound archives in past years has been reel-to-reel. In the last ten years, however, large numbers of sound recordings have been made on tape cassettes, particularly in the nonprofessional sphere. For some archives and libraries, cassettes are now the predominant type of sound-recording collected.

Cassette tapes offer great convenience in recording, storage, and playback. They are compact, easy to use, and they offer reasonable fidelity for many applications, particularly for the recording of speech. They are not suited, however, for long-term storage. Any material contained on cassettes for which long-term

10. Delos A. Eilers, "Polyester and Acetate as Magnetic Tape Backings," *Journal of the Audio Engineering Society* 17 (June 1969): 304–307.

preservation is important *must* be transferred to 1.5-mil mylar-base tape. For material that is ultimately expendable or that is to be kept on a short-term basis, cassettes are acceptable. Cassettes share many of the same requirements for storage as reel-to-reel tape. However, since no long-range expectations can be had for cassettes, the maintenance of these requirements is not so critical as it is for reel-to-reel tape. In many instances, cassettes will be stored in the same environment as reel-to-reel tape, and no special measures will be necessary for their preservation. If a collection consists exclusively of cassettes, environmental conditions should be established as closely approximating those for reel-to-reel tape as possible. As with reel-to-reel, an absence of thermal and hygroscopic cycling is desirable but need not be held within such close tolerances. In no instance, however, should storage temperatures be allowed to exceed eighty degrees F. Winding tension is less of a factor with cassettes than it is with reel-to-reel. A C60 cassette has only about 280 feet of tape inside, compared to a 7-inch reel, which will contain at least 1,200 feet. In addition, cassette equipment operates at a lower tension than reel-to-reel, so there is less of a problem to begin with. For these reasons, it is not essential to store cassettes in a played state. This may be done, however, when it is desired to make optimum use of storage conditions.

When cassettes are to be retained in a sound archives, only those in C60 and C90 lengths should be shelved, and, preferably, only C60s should be. All materials on C120 and C180 cassettes must be dubbed to C60s; C120 and C180 cassettes use a very thin tape that is highly susceptible to fouling and breakage and will permit significant print-through. For these same reasons, C120 and C180 cassettes should never be used during recording. The advantage of greater uninterrupted recording time is more than offset by the danger of fouling or breakage.

In addition to using only C60 and C90 cassettes, it is important to use cassettes of good quality. Not all cassettes have the same internal construction, nor do the tapes have identical recording qualities. As far as construction goes, only cassettes with screw fittings should be used. This means that should fouling occur—and it often does, even with C60s—the screws may be removed and the cassette dismantled for repair. Cassettes without screws—generally the cheaper brands—must be broken open for repair, and they cannot be put back together again.

Cassettes are available with different recording characteristics, depending on magnetic tape coating formula. For speech, ferric oxide is adequate, while chromium dioxide and ferrichrome tapes are better for music and other high-fidelity applications.

Cassettes are usually supplied in plastic boxes. These offer shelving convenience and excellent protection from dust. They should be retained and used for storage. Cassettes without containers must be provided with them. Cassette containers are available from standard library suppliers.

Storage Requirements for Cylinders

Storage of cylinder recordings presents many problems due to their inconvenient, space-consuming shape and the substances of their manufacture. There is disagreement among sound archivists on the best way of storing them.

One of the important collections of cylinders in this country is at the Syracuse University Audio Archives. The curator of this collection, Walter Welch, has proposed the following storage conditions for cylinders:

1. They should be stored end up, or vertically, in boxes large enough to accommodate a dozen or so cylinders. The boxes are fitted with cardboard tubes in the bottom over which the cylinders slip. The tubes act to position the cylinders and prevent them from touching each other. This arrangement permits air to flow freely around the cylinders and is similar to the original cylinder storage boxes.

2. A relative humidity of not more than 10 percent should be maintained. This is for two reasons. First, the wax compounds used to make cylinders provide an attractive food for fungi. These organisms are discouraged by low humidity. Second, the base of the cylinders often contains wood flour. If the flour absorbs moisture, it swells and distorts the geometry of the entire cylinder. This creates surface noise.[11]

The Welch recommendations are interesting, but there is at

11. Welch, "Preservation," p. 91.

least one major practical objection to them: it would be difficult to construct an environment in which a relative humidity of only 10 percent could be achieved and, once achieved, maintained. An additional problem would be that once the cylinders had become acclimated to the low humidity, they could never be removed from it for playing or study without being subject to severe stressing. These extreme conditions, while they may offer theoretical advantages, would appear to be out of the question for most sound archives and libraries.

Provision of suitable storage containers for cylinders is a problem that libraries and archives must work out individually. Cylinder recordings were produced in a wide variety of sizes and shapes. These include diameters of 1 5/16 inches, 2¼ inches, 3¾ inches, and 5 inches and lengths of 4 inches, 6 inches, and 8 inches. Cardboard containers are suitable for cylinder storage provided they can be closed in such a way as to make a dust-proof seal. Ideally, such containers should be made from an acid-free paper. The cylinders themselves should be vertically positioned. This is usually accomplished by providing spindles of a diameter appropriate to the cylinders involved, as in the Welch recommendations. The diameter of the spindles should be somewhat less than the internal diameter of the cylinders so that the cylinders are fully supported by the spindles and do not wobble. Neither should cylinder and spindle be tightly fitted, however. This storage arrangement will prevent damage to the cylinders from possible acid migration or expansion of the spindle. The Rodgers and Hammerstein Archives of Recorded Sound has used polystyrene wine racks for this purpose.[12]

While elaborate packaging and air-conditioning measures can be taken to protect cylinders in storage, at least several major sound archives do not go to these lengths. The Library of Congress, for example, makes no special provisions for the storage of cylinders. The question of cylinder preservation was not gone into by Pickett and Lemcoe, and so there is no scientific study available. Based upon the practical experience of many sound archivists, it would

12. David Hall, "The Rodgers and Hammerstein Archives of Recorded Sound—History and Current Operation," *Association of Recorded Sound Collections—Journal* 6, no. 2 (1974): 25.

appear that, if adequate steps are taken to ensure the physical safety and cleanliness of cylinders and if they are stored in the same basic conditions as shellac disc recordings, there is little reason to expect that they will not be preserved with equal effectiveness as discs.

As with discs, cylinders should be in as clean a condition as possible prior to entering storage. Since it is not safe to expose cylinders to excess moisture, they cannot be washed. Walter Welch has suggested the use of Micro-Pel, a commercial cleaning-and-polishing preparation, for cleaning cylinders (as well as 78s and LPs). Mr. Welch claims that Micro-Pel not only helps clean cylinders, but lubricates them, reducing wear at high frequencies during playback.[13] The use of Micro-Pel is not widespread among sound archives. Micro-Pel contains silicon, and many authorities reject the use of silicon on records on the basis that, once applied, it is very difficult to remove.[14] The permanent alteration of any item in an archival collection violates one of the cardinal principles of preservation practice. The use of Micro-Pel for cleaning cylinders should be undertaken on an experimental basis only. In the absence of other cleaning agents, there would appear to be no effective way of process-cleaning cylinders. The best that can be accomplished is to clean them on an individual basis with a product such as the Watts Disc Preener or a clean velvet cloth.

Because cylinder playback today requires the use of unusual equipment, and because of the fragility of cylinders, as well as the absence of data on their long-term preservation, it is wise to tape the sonic content of all cylinder recordings.

Playback

If sound recordings are to be preserved with maximum effectiveness, the conditions of their use must be made as safe as possible. It is through use that many collections, particularly those in heavily utilized public or music libraries, are most often damaged—adequate control is not maintained over playback oper-

13. Welch, "Preservation," p. 96.
14. Bruce R. Maier, "In Search of the Perfect Record Cleanser," *High-Fidelity* 22 (September 1972): 54.

ations. When sound recordings are not handled correctly or are played on inferior or improperly adjusted equipment, sound quality can be quickly and irreparably destroyed. When, on the other hand, sound recordings are well cared for and played on good equipment, their effective life will be extended. In addition, it is only through the use of good equipment that the full musical or sonic value of recordings can be appreciated. The provision of excellent use facilities can be expensive, both to purchase and install and to maintain. Given the increasing value of rare recordings, the rising price of commercially available discs, and the difficulty, if not impossibility, of replacing out-of-print discs, it is not unreasonable to invest in good playback equipment. When preservation is a serious goal of a library or archive, the best use conditions are essential.

In making use conditions as functional as possible, a unified institutional policy should be developed covering handling and cleaning of sound recordings, playback equipment and its maintenance, and dubbing (transferring to tape) in relation to playback frequency for each major type of sound recording in the collection.

Disc Playback

Discs should be handled as little as possible in the transfer from packaging to turntable and back. It is particularly important to avoid touching groove surfaces with fingers. Oil, which is always present on the skin, when deposited on grooves will attract and hold dust particles. Oil can also serve as a base upon which mold will develop. Discs should be held by fingertip at their outer diameter, supported if necessary with finger tips on the center label, which cannot be damaged by grease.

A convenient way to hold discs and to remove them from wrappers or dust jackets with one hand is to support the disc from underneath with finger tips on the center label and the thumb on the outer edge. The disc can be balanced easily this way, and the other hand is available to stabilize it if necessary or to help remove the inner liner.

An important aspect of disc playback is frequency of use. When a disc is played, it is subject to stress. Because of the small dimensions of the stylus tip, a stylus force of only one gram from a microgroove cartridge produces an enormous pressure against the

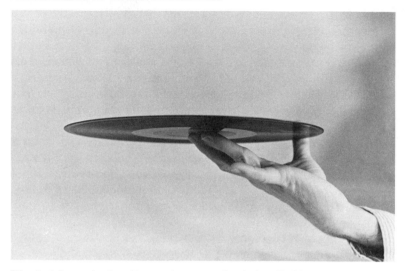

Fig. 5. A long-playing disc can be conveniently handled by supporting the disc from the label by the third and fourth fingers while balancing it at the rim with the thumb. It is important not to touch disc surfaces with fingers. Body oils will attract dust.

groove walls, between 6,000 and 16,000 pounds per square inch. This pressure exists between two objects in relative motion and therefore develops friction, which, in turn, produces high temperatures. Temperatures of up to two thousand degrees Fahrenheit at points of stylus-disc contact may be developed on a long-playing record. This temperature is created for only a fraction of a second. The thermoplastic properties of vinyl and shellac are such that they will not be permanently deformed under those conditions. Nonetheless, significant stress is created. It is for that reason that *no disc should ever be played more than once every twenty-four hours.* This is an important point to observe. The twenty-four-hour interval allows the vinyl or shellac to "relax" after its stressing. It has been found that playing a vinyl disc two times in a row creates the same amount of wear as fifty to a hundred normal

15. Warren ("Blob") Cook, "Paper and Plastic," *Record Exchanger* 4, no. 4 (n.d.): 15, col. 1.

playings spaced sixteen hours apart.[15] When discs must be auditioned more frequently than this, they should be taped and the tapes used for listening.

In addition to controlling frequency of use, record conservators need to keep track of the total number of times a disc is played. Once a disc has been played about ten times, it is a good idea to tape it and play the tape from that point on. That policy is followed in at least one major United States sound archives. There, a small tick-mark is made on the dust jacket of discs each time they are played. After the tenth playing, each disc is taped. (This procedure presents certain legal problems that will be discussed in chapter 4.) Some deterioration of sound quality will occur under the best playback conditions. Taping ensures that that deterioration will be minimized.

Disc Cleaning

When the disc has been placed on the turntable, it is next necessary to clean it. Cleaning the disc prior to, during, and after playback is of vital importance in preserving its sound quality. Dust and other airborne particulate matter will always be present to some degree in a playing environment and will settle on the record surface. A revolving disc, in fact, creates a vortex that draws air down to the disc and out over its surface, acting as a siphon for dust.

Dust particles resting in groove walls will interfere with playback in two ways. First, when the stylus strikes a dust particle, a loud tick will be heard in the reproduced sound. The noise detracts from listening concentration. More seriously, the dust particle may be permanently impacted into the groove wall. That problem is particularly severe for LPs. A microgroove stylus moves at a considerable speed in outer grooves and operates at high pressures and temperatures—conditions sufficient to drive the particle into the vinyl, lodging it there for the life of the disc. In that way, the initial tick will be reproduced each time the disc is played. If discs are not systematically cleaned with each playing, new ticks will continue to be added to the grooves, resulting in a noisy recording filled with ticks and scratches—a situation that makes the listening experience trying or, if the process of deterioration is advanced, impossible.

There are a number of different ways of cleaning discs for playback, and many products are available to help. Some are dangerous for disc surfaces, others are ineffective, while a relative few are useful and safe.

The disc-care products put out by Cecil Watts, Limited, have been on the market for many years. Watts was one of the first people to recognize the need for disc-cleaning before and during playback. Given the fiber technology available at the time the Watts products were introduced, Watts developed both safe and effective cleaning aids. These were intended primarily for use with LPs. They include a preener (a pad made from a velvetlike material for cleaning disc surfaces), various types of parastats (essentially preeners with antistatic capability), the well-known dust-bug (consisting of a podium, arm, and cleaning brushes that track the disc), a stylus-cleaner, and a record-washing brush. Of the many products that have come on the market since the introduction of the Watts preener and dust-bug, only a few do a better job of disc-cleaning.

One of the advantages of the Watts products is that they do not require the use of liquids on record surfaces, as many other systems do. The Watts firm has stated in its instruction brochures that the use of anti-static and cleaning fluids should be avoided on disc surfaces.[16] There is controversy on that point in the audio community. Where the long-range preservation of sound recordings is concerned, a conservative course should be followed and the use of fluids avoided.

For the use of Watts products, good instructions are provided, including some explanation of the theory behind the product design and application. Among other things, Watts points out that separate equipment should be maintained for cleaning LPs and 78s. If that is not done, grit from the shellac surfaces of 78s may contaminate LPs and cause groove damage. The suggestion to use separate equipment is good advice to follow.

Because the Watts products are generally less expensive than other disc-care products, their use might be considered in libraries or other institutions where sound recordings, particularly LPs, are played frequently and do not require maximum cleaning or protec-

16. "Just for the Record," p. 13.

tion. The most useful Watts products are the dust-bug and the parastat. The dust-bug, when set up and deployed properly, is a helpful way to retard the development of ticks in frequently played recordings, while the parastat is a convenient cleaning aid.

Devices similar to the dust-bug are manufactured by several firms. One of the more readily available ones is put out by Audio-Technica, their model AT6002. Like the dust-bug, this device consists of an arm and a dust-collecting brush on a base that mounts on the turntable. The brush and arm track the disc at about the same speed as the pickup (cartridge), removing dust and other particulate matter from the grooves. One problem with devices like the dust-bug is that they can cause a large electrostatic charge to build up on the disc. The Watts dust-bug solves that problem by creating a zone of moisture around the cleaning bristles. That method is not fully successful. If the electrostatic charge is not continuously drained, it will cause dust to adhere to the disc surface even more strongly than it otherwise would. The Audio-Technica dustbug uses a brush made of electrically conductive carbon fibers; the brush, in turn, is grounded to the turntable via a wire. That procedure helps disperse electrostatic charges. This type of dust-bug, while more expensive than the Watts, offers better static reduction and groove cleaning.

Many products of the plush-pad type are available. These are generally made from a velvetlike material and contain a radioactive ion source to help control static electricity. The plush pad is used to wipe the disc clean, usually while the record is rotating on the turntable. Such brushes, although they will cause little immediate harm to discs, are not effective for cleaning, because it is usually impossible to remove the brush from the rotating disc surface without allowing some of the collected dust to fall back on the disc. The problem will be aggravated to the extent that static dispersal is inefficient (which it usually is). The plush-pad type of brush will remove dust and is better than nothing at all, but it does not do its job well.

A more ambitious type of disc-cleaning system is the Discwasher brush. The Discwasher system has been on the market for about eight years. It was developed as the result of a concerted research effort and involved an attempt to formulate scientifically an effective disc-cleaning fluid and develop a suitable cleaning brush. The product has gone through several stages of evolution and is currently called Discwasher III. It consists of a special brush and fluid. The fluid is applied to the brush, which is then held on the rotating disc surface and turned in a special way. The process is supposed to remove dust from the grooves and then trap it on the brush so that the brush can be removed from the disc without redepositing the dust.

The Discwasher system has received favorable notice in the audio press. On the other hand, reservations about its use have been expressed in authoritative quarters. One objection to the Discwasher system is that it requires the use of a fluid. The use of any fluid, regardless of how carefully it is formulated, means that dust, removed from one area of a record and taken into suspension, can be redeposited elsewhere on the record. It is not necessarily true that all dust collected in the fluid will be taken up by the brush. Redeposited dust may then create more of a problem than already existed.

Because the Discwasher system has evolved from a careful research program, it must be given serious consideration. Sound archivists and librarians should determine for themselves, as a result of experiment with duplicate discs, whether it works as claimed and has no deleterious effects. There is probably no question that it could be used in a library where discs were frequently played and long-range preservation was not a main consideration. Its use in such a situation would prolong the effective life of LPs. On the other hand, the relatively high cost of the product might put it out of reach in these applications.

Discwasher makes other disc-care products, including a stylus cleaner and a special version of the Discwasher for 78s. The use of Discwasher fluid is effective for removing detritus from the pickup stylus.

Although a number of authorities have spoken against the use of fluids on discs, one school of thought advocates the exact opposite—that records be played while wet. Several wet-playing systems have been introduced, the most easily available being Lencoclean-L. In wet-playing systems, the fluid—usually a combination of ethyl alcohol and water—is used less to clean the disc than it is to improve the stylus-to-groove relationship and maintain a quieter surface, while discharging static. At least one study has been performed, and published, in which discs were subject to extensive repeated playings using both dry (normal) and wet-playing techniques. The investigators concluded that the wet-playing system caused far less buildup of surface noise than the dry system and preserved high-frequency response.[17] The experiment involved two thousand playings per disc. Dry playing caused noise buildup after only a hundred playings. These findings notwithstanding, the wet-playing system must be regarded as exceptional. Here, as with Discwasher, there may be questions about the ultimate effects of the system. Use should be on an experimental basis. Wet playing may be used, however, to reduce surface noise of very noisy 78s during taping (see chapter 3).

Some disc-cleaning and playing fluids, such as Lenco, contain alcohol. Alcohol-base fluids will not attack vinyl, but because alcohol is a solvent for shellac, the use of such fluids should be avoided on 78s. If wet playing is to be tried with 78s, distilled water is the safest liquid to use.

There are at least two disc vacuums on the market. These are the VacORec and Groovac. VacORec is a free-standing unit into which individual records are inserted. A motor causes the record to rotate and a brush cleans it. At the same time a vacuum system removes the dust. VacORec has received mixed reports. One reviewer in the audio press found it less than satisfactory. On the other hand, a well-known sound archivist has experimented with it and likes it. There would appear to be little that VacORec can accomplish that other, less expensive methods of disc-cleaning cannot accomplish as well, if not better.

Groovac is a device that vacuums the grooves as the disc is played. It is set up on the turntable. A remote suction-pump provides the vacuum. An arm tracks the record and sucks dust off the grooves. The ingenuity of the Groovac system must be admired, but, again, it probably cannot do what less expensive and simpler approaches do just as well.

Some cartridges now include a small brush that cleans the grooves just before the stylus plays them. Stanton cartridges have had this type of brush for some time. A brush has recently been

17. F. A. Loescher, "Record and Stylus: How Long Do They Last?," *Gramophone* 53 (June 1975): 126ff.

introduced on the top-of-the-line Shure cartridge, V-15 Type IV. These brushes are good groove cleaners, but they cannot do as effective a job as other products. They should not be relied upon alone to clean discs.

In addition to most of the above-listed products, which have been developed with a serious view toward record preservation, many antistatic sprays, fluids, and brushes are available, particularly at lower prices. These products are almost certain to cause more problems than they solve, and their use should be rejected. This is especially true for sprays and fluids that are likely to clog grooves and attract dust and other particulate matter.

An unusual disc-cleaning product has recently been introduced by Empire Scientific Company, a manufacturer of cartridges and turntables. It is the Audio Groome Disco Film. Disco Film is a viscous liquid that is spread over the disc surface with a brush. In about one-and-a-half hours, the liquid dries, forming a plastic film. The film is then peeled off and, in theory, a considerable amount of dirt is removed with it. The product has been favorably reviewed in the audio press.[18] Apparently, it does indeed clean dirty LPs, although it cannot be used with shellac discs. However a number of questions remain about its use. Does the peeling-off process effectively remove all the Disco Film, or is there a residue? What are the long-range effects of having treated a disc with Disco Film? The liquid is water-based and therefore should not attack vinyl. In view of the fact that no long-range test results have been published on Disco Film, its use should be considered experimental at this time. A distinct drawback of the product is its cost. One container, priced at $29.95, will clean seventy sides, or thirty-five discs. This works out to be 85¢ per disc.

Perhaps the best all-around combination of products for disc care is the Decca record brush and dust-bug. The Decca record brush consists of many thousands of tiny carbon-fiber bristles. These bristles are soft, very narrow, and electrically conductive. They can reach deep into grooves with safety and remove dust. At the same time, they will conduct static charges away from the disc surface. The amount of dust that the Decca record brush can re-

18. George W. Tillet, "Empire Disco Film Record Cleaner," *Audio* 63, no. 4 (April 1979): 75.

Fig. 6. Discs should be cleaned with a brush prior to playback. The model shown here, by Decca, offers excellent performance. With the turntable rotating, the brush is lightly applied to the disc surface and held stationary while the disc turns. After several rotations the brush, still held against the disc surface, is gradually moved onto the label and lifted. In this manner, most of the dust from the disc is removed. Other brushes will redeposit dust.

move from an apparently clean disc is remarkable. The brush is used on a rotating disc. It is pressed gently against the grooves. When it has collected the dust from the grooves it is gradually moved toward the center of the disc, onto the label, and then removed. In this way, the dust collected by the brush is completely removed from the disc surface and environment. After the disc has been cleaned, the dust-bug is deployed to keep the grooves free of dust during playback. The dust-bug is similar to other devices of this type. It consists of a base and pivot, an arm, and a carbon-fiber brush. The carbon-fiber brush allows static to be discharged through the arm and a ground wire. The absence of static build-up permits dust to be effectively removed and reduces the likelihood of it being attracted to the disc surface. The combination of the two Decca products retails for about thirty-two dollars and is well

Fig. 7. A dust-bug type of record cleaner, such as this one by Decca, should be employed to clean grooves as the disc is played. This method ensures that build-up of groove noise due to impacted dust particles will be kept to a minimum. The procedure will also help to reduce electrostatic charges. Note the ground wire protruding from the left of the dust-bug's base.

worth the cost. While the products were designed primarily for use with LPs and 45s, they may also be used with shellac 78s. It would be a good idea to maintain two sets of disc-cleaning equipment, one for 78s and the other for microgroove recordings. The Decca products are well designed and allow the advantages of the dry-cleaning approach to be realized to the fullest. They are simple and quick to use and appear to have no drawbacks other than cost.

Cleaning of instantaneous recordings presents special problems, due to the sensitive surfaces of these discs. The use of any cleaning product on acetates and nitrates must be accompanied with great care. No brush with stiff bristles (such as the Discwasher) should be used. A light brushing with the Decca record brush is the most that should be attempted, and even that should be avoided if possible.

When a de-staticizing type of dust-bug is not used, static buildup

Fig. 8. Static build-up is a frequently encountered problem with vinyl discs. An excellent way to discharge accumulated static electricity is by means of an antistatic pistol. The pistol is aimed at the disc, which may be rotating or stationary, and the trigger is slowly squeezed several times. This procedure should be followed before and after each playing.

on LPs will be a problem. Static buildup may become a problem anyway, depending on local environmental conditions. The static discharge route of conductive dust-bugs is not always adequate. Discs are electrostatically charged if they produce a crackling sound when removed from the turntable. Electrostatic voltage should be removed from discs, not only because it will cause dust to be attracted to the disc surface, but because, if severe enough, it may also interfere with the performance of the cartridge.

The most effective way of discharging discs is through the use of an antistatic pistol. The original antistatic pistol was developed by Zerostat. It incorporates a quartz element that is alternately stressed and relaxed by the action of the trigger. This procedure releases a positively charged and then negatively charged stream of ions. The combined result is to discharge any electrostatic voltage on the disc. The Zerostat pistol is highly effective at de-staticizing, and its use is recommended. Other de-staticizing pistols are available and will probably do an equally good job. The antistatic pistol is not a rugged device, and care must be exercized to see that it is not dropped or otherwise abused. As a general policy, it is a good idea to de-staticize all LPs before and after use.

One of the most interesting disc-protection products to come on the market in recent years is Sound Guard. Sound Guard is a liquid that can be sprayed onto the surfaces of LPs and 45s via a Freon-type aerosol. The liquid dries, forming a microscopically thin layer of lubricant over the grooves, helping to protect them during repeated playings of the disc.

Sound Guard has been tested and reviewed in the audio press. It has received mostly favorable comment[19] and appears, in certain respects, to work very much as it's supposed to. The major thrust of the published test results has been to demonstrate that the high-frequency response of treated LPs—high-frequency response is the region first affected by repeated playings—was significantly preserved by the use of Sound Guard. Reduction in surface noise buildup also occurs, although here the published results are somewhat less convincing. Application of Sound Guard seems to have no adverse effect on sound quality when treated and untreated discs are compared.[20] Certain problems are inherent in the use of Sound Guard, however, which may make this otherwise very attractive product seem of questionable value in some situations.

To begin with, Sound Guard does not clean or restore discs—it simply protects what is already there. Thus, any dust or other particulate matter already on the groove walls will be encapsulated by Sound Guard and become a permanent feature of the recording. Sound Guard should therefore be used only on records that have been scrupulously cleaned. Second, Sound Guard is not applied with equal success by all users. There have been reports that it is not difficult to apply too much Sound Guard, with the result that the preservative will clog the stylus and cause other problems. Finally, the use of any product that creates a perma-

19. "Sneak Previews—Ball Sound Guard," *The Absolute Sound* 2, no. 8 (Summer/Fall 1976): 415–416.

20. Leonard Feldman, "Effect of Ball Brothers' Sound Guard Lubricant on Frequency Response, Signal-to-Noise Ratio, and Harmonic Distortion Reproduced from Disc Recordings" (Muncie, Ind.: Ball Brothers, 1975).

nent, unalterable change in a physical object runs counter to the best preservation practice. Once Sound Guard is applied, it is there for good. If, for example, there should be long-range harmful effects not yet known, it would in all likelihood be impossible to save the treated discs. The conservative sound archivist would, on those grounds, probably avoid its use at the present time. It should be pointed out that Sound Guard, because of its great potential advantages in disc-protection, is of interest to large sound archives. It has been under test at the Library of Congress.

These are circumstances in which the use of Sound Guard would be indicated. In a library with a circulating or frequently used disc collection, for example, the routine treatment of discs with Sound Guard would have a significant effect on the useful life of discs. In that respect, the low unit-cost of disc treatment would be well worth the investment because of the reduction of disc-replacement cost and improvement in sonic quality.

In addition, Sound Guard is used in at least one major sound archives in the dubbing of acetate recordings. Before an instantaneous recording can be transferred to tape, certain information must be determined about the recording, including the proper transcription speed and equalization. That information can usually be determined only by playing the disc. Sometimes, a number of playings are necessary. Unfortunately, the sound quality of instantaneous recordings deteriorates badly with each playing. Treatment of such acetate discs with Sound Guard has been found to reduce damage to the disc during test playings. A preferred method of accomplishing this is to tape the disc and use the tape for pitching, and so on.

A product similar to Sound Guard is Pro-Disc. Pro-Disc is designed for use with 78s or LPs. In this system, the preservative is a dry film. The disc is placed inside a special container, and the preservative is introduced through a vent by means of a non-Freon gas. Pro-Disc has not received widespread attention in either the audio or archival community and does not appear to have been tested.

Disc-protection products such as Sound Guard and Pro-Disc offer great promise for the preservation of sound recordings. Thanks to a growing awareness of the importance of preserving sound recordings, development is occurring in the field of disc protection. Considerable private research is taking place with future products offering possibly significant advantages over present methods of record-cleaning and preservation. The best present methods of cleaning, however, work well and, when applied systematically and correctly, will extend disc life and sound-quality well beyond what would be obtained with no measures at all. Disc-cleaning is only one of the requirements necessary to achieve optimum preservation. Playback equipment has a direct bearing on disc life as well as sound-quality. It must meet and maintain adequate levels of performance if disc use is to have no adverse effect on life expectancy and retrieval of sonic information.

The disc playback chain consists of the following elements: stylus, cartridge (pickup), tone arm, ·turntable, preamplifier, amplifier, and headphones (or loudspeakers).

Styluses

Of all the components in the disc reproduction chain, it is the stylus, traveling directly in the disc groove, that has the greatest impact on the quality of sound recovered from the disc and on groove life. The shape of the stylus, its dimensions, and the force with which it contacts the groove are the principal variables to be considered (stylus pressure, or tracking force, will be discussed with tonearms).

Stylus tip shape was originally spherical, or conical, and it is that type of stylus that is used for 78s. With the development of the microgroove, and the subsequent ability of manufacturers to produce stylus tips of smaller size and more accurately controlled shapes, it was discovered that there were technical advantages to using an elliptical stylus shape, principally in the reduction of what is called *tracing distortion.* The spherical or conical stylus presents an essentially hemispherical shape to the groove while the elliptical presents an elongated, elliptoid shape. Elliptical styluses are the kind most frequently used today for reproducing LPs. In addition to these two basic types, several new shapes have been introduced, the most significant being the Shibata, or tetrahedral, tip, which was designed primarily for use with microgroove quadraphonic discs. It may be used also with stereo microgroove discs.

There is little disagreement that spherical styluses should be used for 78s. Spherical styluses may be obtained in two forms for this application: truncated and nontruncated. In the nontruncated stylus, the tip extends to a full hemispherical shape. In the truncated stylus, the tip is cut off before it becomes hemispherical. In that way, the stylus rides more on the groove wall than on the groove bottom. When the groove bottom is avoided, so are noise-producing substances such as dirt and shellac detritus that settle there. It has been found that, in playing old 78s, the truncated stylus will often provide better sound quality because of this reduction in noise. Truncations of from 10 percent to 15 percent are commonly used. The use of truncated or nontruncated styluses is a pragmatic decision based on which sounds better. Neither will have an adverse effect on groove life, other factors being equal.

There is disagreement, however, about the effect of the elliptical stylus on groove life. The elliptical stylus presents a smaller surface area to the record groove and therefore exerts greater pressure than a spherical tip tracking at the same force. Although elliptical styluses are by far the more prevalent type available for use with LPs, the spherical-tip stylus remains available for stereo microgroove recordings.

In a series of classic studies done in 1968, J. G. Woodward applied scanning electron microscope techniques to the study of disc surfaces. Photographs taken by Woodward show that, in repeated playings, the spherical tip produces less wear on the groove wall than an elliptical-tip stylus tracking at the same force.[21] Many authorities, including such emminent ones as Robert Carneal of the Library of Congress, have stated that the spherical tip produces less wear.[22] Both the Library of Congress and Rodgers and Hammerstein Archives of Recorded Sound use spherical-tip styluses. Although the spherical tip will produce more wear on the groove wall with the initial playing, wear thereafter is minimal. The elliptical tip continues to wear with each playing. However, at

21. J. G. Woodward, "The Scanning Electron Microscope—a New Tool in Disc-Recording Research," *Journal of the Audio Engineering Society* 16 (July 1968): 258–265.

22. For other opinions in favor of the spherical-tip stylus, see Woodward, "Scanning Electron Microscope," p. 261, col. 1; Cook, "Paper and Plastic," pt. II, p. 19, col. 1; F. A. Loescher and F. H. Hirsch, "Long Term Durability of Pickup Diamonds and Records," *Journal of the Audio Engineering Society* 22 (December 1974): 800.

least one expert has written that, when installed in the correct arm, the elliptical-tip stylus may actually produce less wear than the spherical.[23] The Yale Historical Sound Recordings Collection uses elliptical-tip styluses as well as spherical. The use of spherical-tip styluses in two of the nation's largest sound archives lends a considerable measure of professional support to this procedure. Nonetheless, opinion remains divided among authorities. The use of the elliptical tip for infrequently played LPs will certainly not bring about any serious degradation of sound quality.

Archivists or librarians seeking to employ spherical-tip styluses will find that only a few cartridge manufacturers produce them and that they are not inexpensive. Three such manufacturers are Pickering, Stanton, and Shure. Other cartridges available with the spherical tip include Denon (DL 103 C) and GAS (Sleeping Beauty). The latter two are expensive and, because of their design, require the use of step-up transformers. For practical purposes, therefore, Shure, Pickering, and Stanton are the major United States suppliers. These firms make excellent cartridges. The Shure V-15 Type III G and V-15 Type IV G have been consistently rated as the best-sounding cartridges available by a leading American audio publication.[24]

Stylus diameter will have a significant effect on sound quality where 78s are involved. While the dimensions of styluses for microgroove recordings are fairly standard (.5 to .7 mil for spherical and .3 by .8 mil for elliptical), a considerable range of stylus diameters is necessary for effective playback of 78s. The correct stylus diameter will produce the best fidelity, minimize scratch and hiss, and cause least wear to the disc. Correct stylus diameter is usually determined by trial and error, with sound quality the main guide. This approach requires that a considerable selection of stylus sizes be available.

The Library of Congress uses at least seventy-five different-sized styluses in its sound laboratory, ranging in diameter from .25 mil to 30 mil. Most are concentrated around 3.0, 2.7, 2.5, 2.2 and 1.5 mil. Small differences, even at these microscopic dimensions,

23. J. R. Sank, "Biradial and Spherical Stylus Performance in a Broadcast Disc Reproducer," *Journal of the Audio Engineering Society* 18 (August 1970): 402–406.

24. "Recommended Components," *Stereophile* 4, no. 3 (1978): 32.

can have important results. These stylus sizes were developed by Mr. Carneal in conjunction with Frank Pickering, an important figure in the early days of the American high-fidelity industry. They are manufactured by the Stanton firm for their 400 and 500 cartridges. Stanton is one of the few firms still making this kind of equipment. They are able to supply styluses to fit their cartridges in a range of sizes and truncations.

The large number of stylus sizes used by the Library of Congress is dictated by the nature of their holdings, which include many early 78s of diverse origin. A smaller archive with a more homogenous collection of 78s would not require so many styluses. The standard size of spherical stylus for 78 RPM recordings is 2.5 mil (for discs manufactured from the 1920s through the 1950s). Most archives will find that several styluses in the range of 2.2 mil to 2.7 mil will be adequate, particularly where their collections do not include many early 78s.

Playback styluses of all types require regular maintenance if they are to operate effectively and not damage discs. The two main areas of maintenance are stylus-cleaning and wear-inspection.

As the stylus travels through miles of grooves, it will accumulate dirt on the tip. The dirt may consist of grease or oil, vinyl or shellac particles, dust, or a combination of all these. The buildup of dirt will occur even on discs that have been thoroughly cleaned prior to and during playback. This accumulation is undesirable from several standpoints. First, it will affect stylus performance. When the stylus is encrusted with dirt, it cannot make proper contact with groove surfaces, nor can it respond accurately to groove modulations—situations that will cause playback sound-quality to deteriorate. Second, the accumulation of dirt may cause abrasive damage to groove surfaces, particularly on microgroove recordings. Dirt buildup may easily be observed by examining an uncleaned stylus with a 10X or 20X jeweler's eyepiece. To the naked eye, the stylus will appear unencumbered; but with the eyepiece, the stylus tip will be seen to be covered by a variety of materials.

Good stylus-cleaning procedure will include brushing the stylus lightly with a soft camel's-hair brush before each playing. Care must be exercised not to damage the delicate stylus cantilever

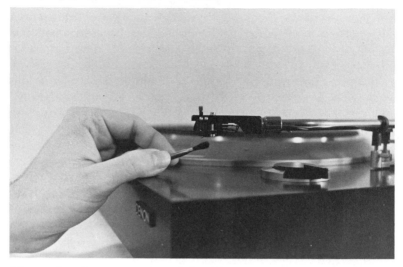

Fig. 9. For the preservation of disc life and to obtain optimum sound quality, it is essential that the stylus tip be clean. A camel's-hair brush, dipped lightly in Discwasher solution, may be used to clean the stylus. A gentle stroking from back to front will normally remove accumulated groove detritus. Care must be exercised not to damage the delicate cantilever mechanism.

during this operation. The cantilever is the thin metal armature on which the stylus is mounted. The correct way to brush the stylus is with a gentle stroke from the back of the cartridge forward. No pressure whatsoever should be exerted upon the cantilever. Several strokes are all that are necessary.

In addition to brushing, the stylus should be cleaned with a solvent. Discwasher solution is excellent for this purpose. The solvent may be placed on a camel's-hair brush or on a stylus-cleaning pad (they are available from Discwasher, Watts, and others) or the brush applied by the cartridge manufacturer. The same gentle stroking motion is used. A drop or two of liquid is usually sufficient. It is important not to allow any excess liquid to remain on the cantilever or to flow back into the cartridge—that will almost certainly ruin the cartridge. Cleaning the stylus-tip with a solvent may be performed once a day, if the stylus is in frequent use, or once a week if it is used less often. The use of a mild solvent is necessary to remove the grease components of accumulated dirt. Discwasher liquid was formulated for that exact purpose; it works well while and at the same time is safe for styluses. Do not use pure alcohol or other undiluted organic solvents to clean the stylus. These may cause the cement bonding the stylus to the cantilever to dissolve, allowing the stylus to rattle in the cantilever or simply to fall off. To check the thoroughness of cleaning, use the jeweler's eyepiece. Some discs will have dirtier grooves than others. In such instances, it may be necessary to clean the stylus after each playing.

Stylus wear must be periodically inspected. The stylus, although made of diamond, is gradually worn by use. When wear reaches a certain point, severe damage to grooves will occur. It is therefore essential not to play discs with a worn stylus. An approximate record should be kept of the number of hours of use logged on each stylus. Cumulative usage should be compared with the manufacturer's suggested stylus life. When hours of use begin to approach that figure, the stylus must be inspected in a properly set-up stylus microscope to determine the extent of wear. Although it has been suggested that it is possible to check stylus wear using a jeweler's eyepiece, that is in fact very difficult to do. A microscope is required. Any dealer in high-quality audio equipment should have a stylus microscope. Unfortunately, not all do, nor do those who do have them necessarily know how to interpret what they see. An attempt should be made to locate a good dealer with a stylus microscope and a qualified technician. If necessary, it is worth paying for an accurate stylus examination. Once damage is done, it cannot be corrected. Large parts of a collection can be quickly damaged from carelessness in respect to worn styluses. Larger sound archives replace styluses routinely. At Rodgers and Hammerstein, for example, all styluses are replaced every six months. Typical stylus life runs from about five hundred to a thousand hours. Some manufacturers claim a life of two thousand hours, but that claim cannot be taken seriously. Inspections at least every five hundred hours are advisable.

A convenient way to keep track of stylus wear is through the use of a stylus timer. Such a timer is manufactured by Pickering & Co. It is their model PST1 Stylus Timer and retails for under fifteen dollars. The stylus timer will clock stylus wear. It has been tested and found to be accurate to within twenty-five hours per thousand hours of stylus use, a very creditable figure.

Cartridges

The type of cartridge selected for disc reproduction will not normally have a significant effect on disc life, providing that it can track at two grams or less. Tracking force is that pressure upon the stylus necessary for the cartridge to follow accurately groove modulations and a certain degree of disc warp. Most modern cartridges are capable of tracking at two grams or less. Among the few exceptions are the Decca line of cartridges and the very expensive EMT moving-coil cartridge. Although both are capable of outstanding performance, neither should be used in a sound archives except for taping purposes only. That applies to any other cartridge tracking at more than two grams. In theory, the lower the tracking force, the less disc wear will occur. If tracking force is too low for the particular cartridge, the stylus will bounce in the groove, also causing groove wear. The Shure V-15 series of cartridges are ideal in this respect. They have excellent tracking ability at about one-gram tracking force.

In addition to tracking force, there are several minor areas in which the cartridge may play a role in groove wear. These are compliance and stylus tip mass. Other things being equal, a cartridge with high compliance and low tip mass should produce less wear—particularly of high-frequency information—than a cartridge with low compliance and high tip mass. Compliance is the ratio of displacement of the stylus to the applied force or, in other words, the freedom with which the stylus can follow groove modulations. Compliance must be carefully controlled, because excessive freedom will introduce distortion. Stylus tip mass is simply the mass of the stylus tip. The lower the mass, the lower the inertia of the stylus and the greater the speed with which the stylus can respond to changes in modulation. In modern cartridges, the difference between the low and high end of these parameters is not great enough to have an important bearing on groove wear.

Choice of cartridge will, however, have an effect on sound quality. Each brand and type of cartridge has a distinct sound of its own, although in many cases this will involve subtle distinctions. Given the limited availability of spherical-tip styluses, cartridge selection may be an academic point. Certainly Shure and Stanton cartridges deliver good sonic results. Other excellent moving-magnet cartridges include the Grace F-8 and F-9 series, the Audio Dynamics Corporation XLM and ZLM series, and the Ortofon M20 series. These are not available with spherical tip, with the exception of the Grace F-9D. Many authorities feel that the moving-coil cartridge offers a significant performance advantage over the moving-magnet cartridge. Improvement, however, comes at a much higher price. While these cartridges—which are structurally the inverse of the more common moving-magnet type—offer greater definition, they are delicate and require the use of a step-up transformer or pre-preamplifier (Denon makes excellent models of both), which adds to their already higher cost. In addition, stylus replacement requires that they be returned to the factory, a major inconvenience. Where requirements for sonic excellence are high and institutional budget allows, experimentation can be made with moving-coil cartridges. In most archival applications, their use will entail unacceptable complications. (It should be pointed out that no moving-coil cartridges are available with 2.5 mil tips for use with 78-RPM recordings. Availability of 2.5 mil tips for moving-magnet cartridges other than Shure, Stanton and Pickering is severely limited.) The greater ruggedness and reliability, lower cost, and more than adequate performance of moving-magnet cartridges of the Shure-Stanton class make them the best choice for the library or archive.

Tone Arms

The tone arm positions the cartridge and stylus over the disc grooves and thus plays a major role in disc preservation. The tone arm must provide the correct tracking force for the stylus, allow it to move freely in both horizontal and vertical planes, provide correct horizontal and vertical tracking angles (angles at which the stylus intersects the groove), and provide compensation for skating force (which tends to draw the cartridge toward the center of the disc).

Tone arms come in two forms—those that are an integral part of a turntable and those that are separate units. Separate units are more expensive and are sometimes difficult to install, but they almost always offer superior performance.

Tracking force has a direct effect on disc wear. If tracking force is too high, the stylus will bear down on the groove walls, causing erosion of subtler modulations and high-frequency information. If it is too low, the stylus will bounce in the groove. Optimum stylus tracking force is normally stated by cartridge manufacturers in their instructions. Actual tracking force should be kept within the manufacturer's range, although experiment will be necessary to determine the point at which performance is best. That will be the point at which the record sounds best.

Most tone arms, whether integrated or separate, will have a tracking-force control with some kind of visual indicator to facilitate adjustment. Such gauges are not reliable. A stylus-tracking-force scale should be kept on hand in any sound archives or record library with which to verify readings on the tone arm. Shure makes an excellent, inexpensive one, their model SFG-2, which retails for less than five dollars and should be considered essential equipment.

Determination of proper tracking geometry of tone arms is a complex problem, one that sound archivists and librarians probably will not wish to deal with. Although technical information has been published on how to adjust optimum horizontal tracking angle for tone arms,[25] the practical problems involved in carrying out the theoretical descriptions are nearly insurmountable. With integrated tone arms, some of the problems have been resolved (or compromised) by the manufacturer and the solutions incorporated in the product. Even so, a number of variables—such as stylus overhang, tone-arm height, and the angle at which the cartridge is mounted in the headshell—will affect performance and disc wear. As a practical matter, manufacturer's installation-and-mounting instructions should be carefully followed. That will insure that horizontal and vertical tracking angle are at least within reasonable bounds.

Vertical tracking angle—that angle with respect to the perpen-

25. Mitchell A. Cotter, "Alignment Procedure for Minimum Lateral Tracking Error Adjustment of Offset Pickup Arms" (Mt. Vernon, N.Y.: Mitchell A. Cotter, ca. 1977).

Fig. 10. The use of a tracking-force scale is recommended to monitor this important aspect of disc playback. The stylus rests in a groove on one arm of the scale. At the opposite end, an indicator is aligned with a stationary marker when the desired tracking force is obtained. The indicator and marker are visible in the small bright mirror to the immediate right of the turntable spindle. The model shown is by Shure.

dicular with which the stylus intersects the disc—has received considerable attention recently, both in terms of its effect on sound quality and disc wear. An industry standard exists for vertical tracking angle—it is fifteen degrees. Cartridges are designed to produce that angle when installed flush in the headshell. Vertical tracking angle may be slightly more or less than fifteen degrees. If it is significantly less—less than zero degrees, for example—the stylus will act as a plow and quickly demolish record grooves. That situation is unlikely to occur in normal use. If the vertical tracking angle is well in excess of fifteen degrees, the stylus will tend to ride higher in the groove and cause groove-wall wear. It is sometimes suggested that the vertical tracking angle be increased for cartridges to improve sound quality. That is accomplished by inserting a shim between the cartridge casing and the headshell. Care should be exercised that the vertical tracking angle is not increased greatly beyond fifteen degrees.

Many tone arms, both integrated and separate, now possess antiskating compensation—usually adjustable by means of a dial calibrated to provide correct compensation for a given tracking force. Such a dial should be carefully set. If it is not, the inner walls of the grooves will be worn more than the outer walls. To test the skating-force adjustment, play a disc. By means of the cueing lever, raise the tone arm. If the stylus remains centered over the groove as the arm is raised, antiskating force is correctly adjusted.

Among separately available tone arms, the English SME series, distributed in this country by Shure, offers good performance, reliability, and reasonable price. SME tone arms are used at the Library of Congress and at Yale. The Grace 707 is also an excellent tone arm, as is the Micro Seiki MA 505.

Turntables

Turntables per se have no immediate impact on disc preservation (although if they include a tone arm, the unit as a whole may be said to have an effect). Turntables, however, play an important part in the disc-reproduction chain and will have a material bearing on sound quality, particularly for 78s. Turntable requirements for 78s and LPs are somewhat different. Because of that, and the fact that few commercially available turntables will play all three principal record speeds (33⅓ RPM, 45 RPM, and 78 RPM), the two types will be treated separately.

The turntable for LPs and 45s should produce a constant and accurate speed of rotation with an absence of low-frequency noise, called rumble, and an immunity to outside vibration or acoustic feedback. Modern technology has made it possible to produce turntables with excellent specifications for speed and rumble, and many are essentially vibration-immune. Rumble is the most expensive problem to solve, and it is the difference between rumble specifications that separates moderately priced from high-priced turntables. Some turntables may possess special features, such as stroboscopic speed indicators, automatic stop and/or variable speed (speed can usually be varied by plus or minus 3 percent, a useful capability), which will somewhat increase price.

Turntables for LPs currently employ two different technologies to couple motor rotation to the turntable platter. One, called belt drive, uses a neoprene belt to connect the motor to the turntable platter. The other system is direct drive, in which the motor shaft is coupled directly to the platter. Both types, when well designed and manufactured, will produce excellent results. Among lower-priced units, direct drive may offer better performance and reliability.

A turntable that is frequently used in record libraries is the Acoustic Research AT–77XB, a moderately priced turntable with belt drive and tone arm and a reputation for trouble-free operation. It does not have unusually low rumble figures, but is adequate in noncritical situations. The low end of the Technics line of turntables also offers good performance at moderate price. These are available in both belt or direct drive and include tone arm.

Among moderate-to-expensive turntables, Thorens and the high end of the Technics series are good choices. Thorens is belt-drive; Technics, direct-drive. Technics is available with or without tone arm, and both offer three-speed models, an important consideration if only one turntable is to be used in an archives. Technics model SP–10 Mark II is without tone arm. Thorens model TDC–126C includes tone arm. The high-end Technics series have a reputation for extreme ruggedness.

The German firm of EMT makes an excellent line of three-speed turntables. These include tone arm. They are very expensive and, although used in some sound archives, such as Rodgers and Hammerstein and Library of Congress, are not necessary for good playback of LPs and 45s.

Probably the best turntables currently available for 33⅓-RPM and 45-RPM discs are the Denon DP-6000 and DP-2000 series. Although expensive (they are priced at approximately $1,000 and $500, respectively), they offer exceptional speed stability, high torque, and very low rumble. The DP-6000 has adjustable speed; the DP-2000 does not. Both types are available with or without tone arm. The tone arm adds to the cost.

While 78s have essentially the same turntable requirements as LPs—low rumble and constant speed—the situation is complicated by the fact that some 78s, particularly early ones, were not recorded at uniform speeds. In addition, some collections will include 78s on sixteen-inch- and twenty-inch-diameter discs. These may require the use of large platters. Unfortunately, it is very difficult to control rumble on large turntable platters.

In a collection with few sixteen-inch discs, the use of Technics or Thorens turntables with 78 RPM speed will probably prove satisfactory. Speed can be varied on the Thorens within limits to allow for different original recording speeds. The occasional sixteen-inch disc can be played on a twelve-inch platter, usually, with no serious ill effects. Richard Warren at the Yale archives has successfully used this technique.

Where greater variation in speed is required, several approaches are possible. In one, a turntable with a synchronous motor is driven by a variable-frequency audio oscillator and amplifier (this method is used at Rodgers and Hammerstein). The synchronous motor responds to the frequency generated by the oscillator and thus can be controlled over a wide range of speeds. Because many modern turntables are not driven by synchronous motors, this technique is of limited applicability.

A less complex approach involves the use of a variable-speed tape recorder, such as the Revox A700. In this method, the disc is played at the nearest correct speed and taped. The speed of the tape can then be adjusted to provide the desired pitch. The Revox A700 can provide a continuously variable tape speed, in three ranges, from two to twenty-two IPS, a span of about 3½ octaves, far in excess of what would ever be required. This method is used at the Library of Congress and at Yale. One of the most difficult tasks faced by the sound archivist is the determination of pitch for old recordings. Variable-speed tape decks provide the most flexible way of dealing with determination of pitch.

When a collection has many sixteen-inch-diameter discs, the use of a transcription turntable (one with a sixteen-inch platter) may be necessary. Because sixteen-inch discs are no longer produced, few manufacturers continue to make transcription turntables. Most sound archives rely on the use of older machines. These must often be rebuilt or extensively modified to provide adequate performance. At the Library of Congress, for example, Gates, Rek-o-kut, and RCA transcription turntables are used. Rodgers and Hammerstein has Fairchild turntables, and Yale has a QRK. None of these are manufactured today. Sound archivists have found all of these machines unsatisfactory in one way or another. The Library of Congress does have, however, an EMT transcription turntable capable of excellent performance, EMT model 927.

It is very expensive (about four thousand dollars) and includes a tone arm and its own electronics. It has very low rumble, the major problem with sixteen-inch turntables.

If the original sonic quality of a disc recording is to be accurately reproduced, the electrical signals generated by the cartridge must be correctly amplified and processed. Processing may involve simple reverse equalization, as with modern LPs, or several stages of filtering and equalization, as with shellac and acetate 78s. The equipment used in this part of the reproduction chain—preamplifier, filter, equalizer, and amplifier—has an important influence on the ultimate sound and its fidelity to the original source. It should be carefully chosen. Good electronic equipment will introduce no unnecessary noise or distortion.

Preamplifiers

It is the function of the preamplifier to raise the output level of the cartridge (1 to 5 millivolts) to a voltage sufficient to drive the amplifier (1 to 1.5 volts). In addition, the preamplifer may be called upon to provide reverse equalization, perhaps its most difficult task.

Equalization began to be applied in the recording industry with the development of electrical recording in 1925. Electrical recording brought about a substantial increase in frequency response. With lateral cutting, however, certain difficulties arose. Low frequencies, if too powerful, could cut into adjacent grooves, while high frequencies, if not powerful enough, would make an inadequate impression on the cutting medium. Compensation was therefore applied to the signal, the high end boosted and the low end attenuated. In order to reproduce the original signal, reverse equalization must be applied.

One of the problems facing the playback engineer is to determine the nature of the required reverse equalization. For LPs made after the industry-wide adoption of the RIAA standard (June 1953), the exact compensation is known. All modern preamplifiers incorporate RIAA compensation in their phonograph amplification circuits, although some are more accurate in that respect than others. Prior to industry-wide adoption, different manufacturers used different equalization schemes. In many instances, these are known, particularly in regard to long-

playing records. For 78s, the picture is less clear—some equaliza-
tions are known, and some are not. Today, specialty preamplifiers
are available that will provide early LP and 78 compensation. It is
also possible to obtain older equipment that has this compensation
available. Otherwise, a variable level, octave or ⅓-octave equalizer
must be employed.

Some turntables, such as EMT, may have built-in preamplifiers.
Most will not. Among preamplifiers for RIAA-compensated LPs,
the All-Test Devices model ATD–25 offers excellent performance
at a reasonable price. The ATD–25 is a basic phonograph
preamplifier and has no control functions. It provides RIAA compensation only. Other low-priced preamplifiers with control functions include the Dynaco models PAT–4 and PAT–5 and the
David Hafler DH–101. These are all good values. The David
Hafler has probably the most accurate RIAA reproduction of any
preamplifier currently on the market. Preamplifiers for LP reproduction can run into a great deal of money. In many applications, a
product such as the Dynaco PAT–4 will be fully acceptable. It
contains a headphone output jack so that no external amplifier is
necessary. Among high-quality phono preamplifiers with excellent
records for reliability may be mentioned the DB Systems DB–1
and the Audio Research SP–3a–1 (recently discontinued) and its
successor, SP–6.

For preamplifiers with other than RIAA compensation, choices
are limited. The Library of Congress uses a HACO (Holzer Audio
Engineering Company) preamplifier that provides a number of
different equalization curves. Rodgers and Hammerstein uses a
Pultec C–2 preamplifier that also offers a choice of equalization
curves. At Yale, one of the last available tubed McIntosh
preamplifiers is used. The McIntosh offers a number of possible
equalization settings. The use of good-quality older equipment is
an ingenious way around the problem. When old equipment of this
type is found, it will, in most instances, require rebuilding because
aging electronic components will have an adverse effect on sound.
Even so, the cost of buying used equipment and having it rebuilt
may be less than that of buying new equipment. When buying used
equipment, it is wisest to stay with reliable manufacturers such as
McIntosh, Marantz, Dynaco, Fisher, and Harmon/Kardon. The
Dynaco PAS-3 (no longer manufactured), when properly modified,

is regarded by some as one of the best preamplifiers available. The Audio Dimensions firm of San Diego, California, performs such modifications and also offers kits for that purpose. It is worth noting that older electronic equipment will usually employ tubed amplifying circuits (as opposed to solid-state). Tubed circuits have certain advantages over solid-state, including greater ruggedness and reliability, greater ease of servicing, and generally much higher overload capacity (important when playing 78s and when high-output cartridges are used.) Tubed circuits have disadvantages, however, the principal ones being higher noise level, susceptibility to microphonics (the transformation of physical vibration into electronic signals that intrude upon the program material) and a conceivable future tube shortage. Neither tubed nor solid-state circuits are inherently superior, although some of the finest audio equipment yet produced has employed tubed circuits.

Graphic Equalizers and Filters

An alternate method of providing equalization is through the use of a graphic equalizer. A graphic equalizer divides the frequency spectrum into a number of segments, usually twelve or thirty-six, depending on whether it is an octave or ⅓-octave type. The level of energy passing through each band can be individually controlled. With the use of such equipment, an infinite number of curves can be provided. Equalization is selected either on the basis of listening or on experience with discs of similar manufacture. Among equalizers commonly used in sound archives are Gotham (at Library of Congress), UREI (at Rodgers and Hammerstein), and Altec (at Yale). The Dynaco SE–10 offers excellent quality at a comparatively low price but is an octave equalizer only. Other excellent octave equalizers are the Soundcraftsmen models RP2201-R and RP2215-R, priced at $300 and $370, respectively. All equalizers introduce some form of phase distortion and noise into the processed signal, as do most compensated phonograph preamplifiers. Some products are better in these respects than others. The Dynaco equalizer and Hafler preamplifier offer highly linear, low-noise performance.

The graphic equalizer may also be used to provide the frequency-response modification necessary for diameter equalization. Many electrical 78s were engineered with diameter equalization in which the intensity of the recorded signal was increased as the cutting head neared the center of the disc. This process was followed to improve high-frequency performance. Reverse equalization is most conveniently obtained using a graphic equalizer.

Early electrical shellac and acetate recordings were produced with unsophisticated electronic and mechanical equipment. Many discs from the 1920s and '30s, when played on modern equipment, will be found to have serious audible forms of noise. This is particularly true for instantaneous recordings, which were often made on low-quality equipment. The most common forms of noise encountered on these discs are rumble (from poorly engineered turntables) and 60-Hz hum (from poorly filtered electronic circuitry). The most effective way of eliminating this noise during playback (and taping) is through the use of a filter set. A filter set consists of a tuneable filter, the frequency of which is continuously variable over the audible-frequency spectrum. The type of filtering desired is also adjustable—that is, notch-filtering or more gradual slopes. A filter set can easily be adjusted to remove 60-Hz hum and the audible harmonics produced by this frequency. The most popular filter set currently in use in archives is the UREI model 565.

Amplifiers

The function of the amplifier is to increase the voltage of the signal delivered by the preamplifier and to provide adequate power to drive headphones or loudspeakers. The amplifier should not introduce distortion. In the context of the sound archive or record library, amplifier power need not be great. Thirty watts, in most instances, is fully adequate. What is important is an open sound quality, low noise, and absence of distortion.

A moderately priced, low-distortion amplifier with an outstanding record for reliability is the Crown model D70. This amplifier includes level controls and a headphone jack. It is in use in many broadcast studios and other professional situations. Another good basic amplifier is the GAS Grandson of Ampzilla, which, despite its name, is an excellent performer and reasonably priced. It does not include level controls or a headphone jack. Its reputation for reliability is unestablished. Two Dynaco products no longer manufactured but of excellent quality are the Stereo 70 amplifier (tubed) and the Stereo 120 amplifier (solid-state).

Headphones and Loudspeakers

The final stage in the audio reproduction process will either be headphones or loudspeakers. In most sound archives or record libraries, headphones are used because they minimize disturbance to others. Open-air headphones (which can be heard by nearby persons) and loudspeakers may be used when this is not a consideration. Some headphones—the low-impedance type—do not require a separate power amplifier. Others, including electrostatics and high-impedance types, require an amplifier. All loudspeakers require a power amplifier.

Among the closed type of headphone, the low-end Koss line offers good value. The best known model here is the PRO–4AAA (low impedance). The Beyer DT–240 and AKG 240 are good intermediate-priced headphones. For critical applications, the STAX SRX Mk I or Mk II will provide greater accuracy than the most expensive speaker systems available. They are open-air and are of the electrostatic type. They require a power amplifier, such as the GAS Grandson of Ampzilla, for operation.

A good, low-priced monitor loudspeaker is the EPI model 100. The Rodgers/BBC LS 3/5a, in the medium-priced class, offers outstanding reproduction. It was developed by the BBC for broadcast monitoring. These speakers are quite small and can be easily situated in confined quarters. More elaborate speakers than these will almost never be required in a sound archives or record library.

For purposes of auditioning and/or patron playback, the choice of headphones or loudspeakers will probably be dictated by the physical set-up of the listening facilities. However, for purposes of monitoring, particularly during taping, equalization, filtering, and so on, it may be preferable to use loudspeakers. Loudspeakers are customarily used by recording engineers for this purpose because they provide a more natural listening experience than headphones and provide conditions that relate more closely to the circumstances under which the recording will ultimately be played. For that purpose, the Rodgers speakers are ideally suited.

Tape Playback

One of the principal advantages of tape over disc as a medium of recorded sound is its comparative freedom from use-associated problems. For example, under normal conditions, tape will never require cleaning during recording or playback. If it is used in the kind of environment earlier described, it is unlikely that it will ever accumulate enough dust to interfere with sonic quality, regardless of frequency of use. Also, tape undergoes far less serious deterioration of sound quality with repeated playings than discs. A tape can be played at least a hundred times with little, if any, noticeable deterioration. To achieve this for an LP would require carefully controlled use conditions.

While tape has these advantages, it is not without drawbacks. It is more awkward to use than discs, requiring winding and threading, and has some special handling needs that must be observed if sonic quality is not to be diminished (many of these problems are eliminated in the tape cassette format). In addition, tape equipment must be periodically cleaned, demagnetized, and aligned if optimum performance is to be attained and tapes not damaged. Tape equipment on an hours-of-use basis probably requires more attention than does disc equipment. Nonetheless, the advantages of tape over presently available disc technology are such that it must be considered the preferred form of sound recording for archives and libraries.

Handling

As with any type of sound recording, handling of tape should be kept to a minimum. Excessive handling will result in grease and oils being deposited on the tape surfaces. Dust particles will then tend to accumulate on these areas, increasing the possibility of dropout.

Unless tape is being edited or otherwise specially processed, most handling will occur when tape is threaded into the machine. Handling problems at this stage can be largely eliminated by the use of leader tape. A leader tape is a short piece (about six feet) of nonmagnetic tape attached to the beginning and the end of the tape. It serves a number of functions. First, it ensures that only the leader is handled during threading, which keeps the main tape clean and prevents the ends from becoming frayed with repeated use. Second, it prevents the main tape from being damaged should the tape machine not be stopped in time in fast-forward or rewind modes. When the end of the reel is reached in high-speed transport, the tape will be whipped around the tape guides. When leader is used, the main tape will not be subject to that stress. Leader tape should be attached to the beginning and end of all reels of tape that do not have it. Many tapes will already have leader attached, particularly amateur or audiophile-quality tapes of recent manufacture. In such instances, the type of leader employed is often mylar or some other plastic. The preferred form of leader tape, however, is paper. It is available in rolls from most suppliers of professional recording tape and is attached using normal splicing techniques. Leader is not required on cassette tapes.

A major problem with the magnetic-tape medium is the phenomenon called *print-through*. Print-through occurs when one layer of tape transmits some of its magnetic information to an adjacent layer of tape. Print-through is a function of several variables, including tape tension, tape coercivity, tape thickness, and temperature. When 1.5-mil tape is handled at normal tension, print-through will be minimized. High-coercivity tape (metal-particle tape) will also minimize it. Finally, temperature, both in storage and handling, must be kept within limits or print-through will be significantly increased.[26] It has already been mentioned that storage temperatures for tapes should not be allowed to exceed 80 degrees Fahrenheit. It is a frequently overlooked point that the temperature on top of a tape machine may significantly exceed that figure. The heat generated by electronic circuitry and transport motors may reach temperatures as high as 150 degrees Fahrenheit on top of some professional tape decks. For that reason, tapes should not be left on tape machines any longer than is necessary. Their prompt removal after use will reduce temperature-induced print-through.

Modern 1.5-mil mylar-base tapes will not present any handling problems, once on the tape machine. When tape machines are operating properly, breakage or other damage to tape is unlikely. Certain inferior tape decks may cause tape breakage. The use of such equipment should, of course, be rejected. Older acetate-base tapes, however, if sufficiently deteriorated, may begin to crack or

26. Wilfried Zahn, "Preservation and Storage of Tape Recordings," *Phonographic Bulletin* 15 (July 1976): 5–6.

may even break when played. That should be anticipated when such tapes are played. The use of a tape deck with particularly gentle tape-handling characteristics may be required. At the Library of Congress, 3M tape decks have been found to work well with older acetate-base tapes.

From time to time, tape editing or splicing will be necessary. Splicing is used to attach leader tape or repair a broken tape. Editing can be used to remove unwanted portions of a tape or otherwise rearrange the sequence of recorded materials. Editing and splicing should be carefully performed, or winding problems will develop.

Splicing should only be done on an aluminum splicing block, of the type sold by professional recording-equipment suppliers. The kind of splicing kits available in stereo stores are not suitable for serious work. A professional splicer is preferable. In addition, only professional splicing tape should be used. In no circumstances should Scotch tape be used. The adhesive from Scotch tape will spread, causing adjacent layers of tape to stick together. Finally, the use of any iron or steel equipment in contact with the tape during editing or splicing should be avoided. If such equipment is required, it must be demagnetized prior to use to avoid possible damage to the magnetic information on the tape.

Maintenance of Tape Equipment

Tape equipment needs periodic maintenance if maximum playback quality is to be achieved. Major areas of maintenance include cleaning, demagnetization, and replacement of pinch rollers. Other areas are alignment of magnetic heads, adjustment of tape tension, replacement of worn heads, and adjustment of bias and equalization. The latter operations would normally be performed by technical personnel.

When tapes are played, abrasion causes small amounts of the magnetic coating to come off. The coating is deposited in a thin layer on the surfaces with which the tape is in contact. Sometimes this deposition can be seen as a reddish-brown powder. With modern tapes, the residue may be gray or white and is often difficult to detect with the naked eye. It is, nonetheless, there. It will cause uneven tape motion and dropout. If enough accumulates on the magnetic heads, it may cause partial loss of signal.

In order to control the deposition of magnetic coating, tape machines should be cleaned each eight hours of use. Parts to be cleaned are magnetic heads, the capstan (the revolving metal shaft that drives the tape), the pinch roller (the rubber wheel that presses the tape against the capstan), tape guides and lifters (the metal parts that direct the tape across the heads and lift it from the heads during high-speed transport), scrape-and-flutter filters (the round metal rollers over which the tape passes), and the tape-tension arms.

These parts may be cleaned using Q-tips and denatured alcohol or Freon TF. Alternately, cleaning kits are available from manufacturers such as SONY, TEAC, Nortronics, and so on. The kits are more expensive in the long run. All metal surfaces with which the tape comes in contact should be swabbed with a Q-tip that has been dipped lightly in alcohol or Freon TF. Particular attention should be given to the magnetic heads. These must be kept scrupulously clean if good performance is to be obtained. Sometimes it will be possible to see the removed iron oxide accumulations on the Q-tip, although they are not always visible. Even if the oxide cannot be seen, it should not be assumed that the heads did not need cleaning. Cleaning should be carried out as standard operating procedure. For cleaning the rubber pinch roller, it is preferable not to use alcohol, but to use, instead, one of the specially formulated rubber cleaners available for this purpose from the above sources. The pinch roller does not need to be cleaned as often as the tape heads. For cassette equipment, special cleaning cassettes (available from Nortronics and TDK) can be inserted into the deck and played as a tape would be played. These give satisfactory results.

Tape heads, as well as metal parts that the tape contacts, are subject to magnetization. Magnetization of these parts imposes a threat to the sonic integrity of the tape. If severe enough, magnetization will cause partial erasure. For that reason, demagnetization is a standard part of tape-machine maintenance.

Demagnetization is accomplished by the use of a device that produces a magnetic field capable of neutralizing magnetic polarity on the metal parts of the tape deck. When energized, the demagnetizer is slowly brought into proximity with each metal part and then withdrawn. This operation creates a random alignment of magnetic polarities and has the effect of eliminating an over-all magnetic charge. Demagnetizers are available from most of the same suppliers who carry head-cleaning kits or from professional recording-equipment suppliers. Tape recorder manufacturers' recommended frequency of demagnetization suggestions should be observed. Demagnetization may be performed at intervals of about every forty hours of operation. Special battery-powered demagnetizer cassettes are available for use with cassette equipment (TDK makes one). For cassette decks, as well as reel-to-reel, demagnetization is an essential part of maintenance.

The effect of improper tape tension on the storage life of magnetic tapes has already been discussed. It is normally possible to tell by visual inspection whether winding tension is within acceptable limits. Correct tension will produce a smooth, even wind in play or record mode, with no ridges or other irregularities. If incorrect tension is suspected, the problem usually must be referred to a technician. If machines are serviced at regular intervals, tape tension should be inspected at these times.

Accurate magnetic recording and reproduction requires that the magnetic heads be properly aligned in relation to the tape. Alignment takes place along several axes, and screwdriver adjustments are provided on most head assemblies for this purpose. Alignment of heads is set at the factory, and normally will not require readjustment unless the heads have been changed or the tape machine subjected to physical shock. When tape machines are serviced, however, it is a good idea to have the alignment checked, because incorrect alignment will cause reduced output and distortion. For most tape machines, alignment of playback heads can be checked using a test tape. Record heads require the use of a signal generator. Some cassette tape decks—among them Nakamichi and Tandberg—have built-in alignment test equipment, an important and useful feature. Alignment on cassette decks is more critical than reel-to-reel decks due to the narrowness of the tape (and hence the recording tracks).

Magnetic heads are subject to wear caused by the passage of tape. Head wear is a gradual process. Modern magnetic heads are made of highly durable material. Nonetheless, if tape decks are used intensively, tape heads should be inspected for signs of wear.

If wear can be seen with the naked eye, audio performance may have already begun to deteriorate. Worn heads can be refinished, but it is preferable to have new ones installed. This is an expensive job and can be performed by only a skilled technician or factory-service center.

Correct adjustment of bias and equalization is one of the most difficult aspects of tape-recorder maintenance. Bias is a high-frequency alternating current applied to the tape with the recording signal to help compensate for the nonlinearity of the magnetic recording medium. Equalization, as with disc recording, consists of deliberate changes in the level of the signal in recording and playback, to compensate further for this nonlinearity. When bias and equalization are correctly set, what goes into the recorder should be essentially identical to what comes out. Unfortunately, the bias and equalization situation in tape recording is quite complicated. There are trade-offs involved in setting bias and equalization, depending on which aspects of performance (high-frequency response versus headroom, for example) are to be most emphasized. In addition, although a uniform equalization standard exists (NAB, the National Association of Broadcasters), different formulations of tape require different degrees of bias and equalization to achieve the performance standards specified by NAB. This is due to the variation in magnetic characteristics with each oxide (or metal) formulation. While test tapes are available to help in the adjustment procedure, standard test tapes, such as Ampex and Taber, do not always produce identical results. To put it another way, a tape recorded on a carefully set up, properly adjusted machine will not necessarily sound the same when played back on another equally well-set-up machine, or even on a machine adjusted in conformity to test tones recorded on the original machine. More and more commentators have addressed themselves to this problem.[27]

Unpredictability of tape reproduction affects the ability to retrieve sonic content accurately. This fact is of importance not only within individual archives and libraries, but when archives exchange tapes with each other. At the present time, there does not

27. "Better Recordings: a Progress Report," *Stereophile* 3, no. 11 (Winter 1975/1976): 36, col. 1–2.

appear to be a fail-safe solution to the problem of bias and equalization settings. The best procedure for an individual archives or library to follow is to have tape recorders in its facilities biased to one type of tape and to attempt to use that tape consistently (it must, of course, be a tape that is acceptable in other respects). That way, there will be a reasonable degree of sonic consistency for recordings made within the archives. When recordings are sent outside the archives, it is a good idea, if technically possible, to include standard test tones at the beginning of the tape so that tape machines on the other end can be adjusted for accurate reproduction. Typical test tones include 15 kHz for head alignment, 10 kHz and 5 kHz for high-end equalization, and 80 Hz and 40 Hz for low-end equalization, all recorded to give a 0 VU playback level. Inaccuracy in the response of received tapes that do not have test tones can be compensated for by the use of a graphic equalizer, as can tapes recorded at other than the NAB standard or those which, for various reasons, do not conform to that standard.

Recommended Tape Equipment

The selection of tape equipment employed in a sound archives or library should be given careful consideration. Tape machines will be used not only to play already-recorded tapes, but to dub discs and other tapes onto archival storage tapes. Good equipment is essential if original sound quality is to be preserved.

Reel-to-reel tape decks are often divided into three grades: professional, semiprofessional (audiophile), and consumer. Sound archives would normally use only professional or semiprofessional equipment, while good consumer-grade equipment is adequate in most libraries.

Professional tape equipment is characterized by ruggedness of construction, high reliability, and flexibility of operation. There is often no significant difference in performance between professional and semiprofessional equipment. The considerably greater cost of professional equipment is usually justified where tape decks are to be in heavy, continuous use and where reliability and ease of servicing are major factors.

The most frequently found professional-grade tape decks in American sound archives are Ampex, 3M, and Scully. Crown tape decks may also be encountered (though these are no longer manufactured), as well as Studer (a German firm, but their equipment is also manufactured in Tennessee).

Ampex was the first company to market high-quality tape equipment in the United States and has maintained pre-eminence in this field. The Ampex 300 series, widely found in recording and broadcast studios although no longer manufactured, is noted for its ruggedness and reliability. Many Ampex tape decks from the 1950s and 1960s are still in use today. Ampex equipment is used at the Library of Congress and at Rodgers and Hammerstein. Because of improvements in electronic drive and amplification circuitry since the 300 series was introduced, many older Ampex units are retrofitted with new audio and transport-control units. The best-known supplier of these conversion units is Innovonics. The Library of Congress Ampex 300 series decks are equipped with Innovonics 375 amplifiers. Ampex has recently introduced a new line of professional decks, the best of which is their model ATR–102. This machine, in the opinion of some, represents the current state-of-the-art in analogue magnetic-recording technology. It is priced accordingly (about six thousand dollars).

Scully tape decks, manufactured by a firm well known for its disc-recording equipment, are used at both the Library of Congress and Rodgers and Hammerstein. The Scully decks have a reputation for smooth tape handling. The Library of Congress also uses 3M tape decks. This machine has particularly gentle tape-handling characteristics. Its usefulness in playing deteriorating acetate-base tapes has already been referred to.

Crown tape decks have enjoyed a reputation for ruggedness and have often been used for on-location recording. Studer decks are primarily designed for use in recording studios. They are typically supplied in multitrack formats.

For field recording, several makes of excellent miniature reel-to-reel tape decks are available. These include Uher (the least expensive), Nagra, and Stellavox. These machines are lightweight, offer battery operation, and are capable of high-quality performance.

Professional tape decks, because they are installed in a wide variety of situations, are usually not supplied with cabinets or uniform input and output connections. These are normally ordered as optional equipment. In addition to its greater initial cost, therefore, professional equipment will require support and interconnect facilities. One of the advantages of semiprofessional equipment is that it can, in most instances, be unpacked and put into operation immediately.

Probably the two most widely used semiprofessional tape decks are the Revox models A77 and A700. Revox equipment is known for its high quality of construction and outstanding performance. These decks are not considered to be rugged machines (they cannot tolerate physical abuse), but when used under normal conditions will give many years of trouble-free operation. The A700 is the more sophisticated machine. It offers three-speed operation and a continuously variable range of speeds from two to twenty-two IPS, a very useful feature. Both machines will accept 10½-inch reels and are available with many professional options. Yale uses both Revox models.

Other contenders in the semiprofessional class include the Tandberg 20A, which can utilize the new metal particle tapes, and the high end of the Sony and TEAC lines. Tandberg has outstanding performance. Sony decks are known for their reliability.

Semiprofessional decks interconnect using standard RCA phono plugs and high-impedance line-level output and input circuits. This means that installation and compatibility of equipment is not likely to be a problem.

Among consumer-grade reel-to-reel decks, Sony and TEAC represent good value. These machines are well designed and well constructed, are durable, and will withstand some user abuse. In the audiovisual class, Sony offers a complete line of tape decks that enjoy widespread use in libraries. These are adequate for tape playback.

An important consideration when selecting tape equipment is head configuration. Professional stereo recording is customarily done with ½-track heads (for basic 2-channel recording). This format offers performance superior to that of the ¼-track format. Since work in any sound archives should be carried on in as professional a manner as possible, the use of ½-track reel-to-reel tape machines is preferred. On the other hand, archives must contend with the fact that their collections may include substantial numbers of ¼-track recordings. While ½-track stereo recordings may be played on ¼-track stereo equipment, ¼-track stereo recordings may not be played on ½-track tape decks. Either both types of equipment must be kept on hand, or a tape deck with interchangeable heads obtained. Few such machines exist. Fortunately, the Revox A-700, an outstanding performer in almost every respect, is available with interchangeable heads, a fact that would seem to point to this tape deck as the best choice when only one high-quality machine can be purchased. Music libraries and other high-use institutions will probably prefer to employ ¼-track machines, due to their greater tape economy. Most audiophile, or semi-professional, tape equipment is available in either ½-track or ¼-track format, including products from Sony, TEAC, and Tandberg. An alternative to purchasing a machine with interchangeable heads would be to have two tape decks, one a ½-track and the other a ¼-track.

The growing popularity of cassette recording has meant that sound archives and libraries find themselves increasing their holdings in that format. Some disadvantages of the cassette format—including poor long-term storage potential and generally lower sound quality—have already been described. Unless high-performance cassette decks are used, poor sound quality is almost always the result. Low sound quality is tolerable when speech is recorded; it is far less so where music is involved. Sound archives and other institutions should obtain the best cassette equipment they can afford, if music is to be recorded.

Perhaps the leader in the cassette field is the Nakamichi firm. Nakamichi has pioneered in many of the technical developments that have made high-quality cassette recording feasible. Where portable cassette equipment is concerned, their Model 550 is an excellent choice. Model 550 is a stereophonic cassette recorder that can operate on either batteries or alternating current. Results will probably be as good as those obtained by miniature reel-to-reel equipment. It should be noted, however, that cassette equipment of this type cannot be considered to have the same reliability and ruggedness of construction as portable professional reel-to-reel equipment.

For nonportable equipment, Nakamichi 600 and 700 series are good, as are Tandberg TCD 340 and Denon DR–750. These machines are of semiprofessional grade. Where consumer-grade cassette equipment is to be used, the Kenwood KX–1030 and Harmon-Kardon 1500 are good choices.

Where only speech is to be recorded—as, for example, in oral history projects—the use of battery-powered monophonic cassette units is possible. Several Sony models of that type are available. They are reliable and effective for this limited application.

When live recordings are to be made, the use of good microphones is mandatory. The microphone is the most important link in the recording chain. When it is inadequate to the task at hand, there is no way a successful recording can be made. Sony condenser microphones are excellent choices where music is to be recorded. Model C–37 is among the best of this line. Sony electret microphones (also referred to as condenser microphones, but operating on a slightly different principle than true condenser microphones) may be used in less demanding situations. These are available in a wide variety of prices and models.

Good-quality tape is required to produce satisfactory results from recording equipment. Not only is tape quality important, but tape must be matched to the capabilities of the machine with which it will be used. Manufacturer's instruction booklets will specify the correct type of tape to be used for each type of equipment. Such booklets may also specify the exact brand and description of the tape for which the machine was biased.

Tape, for both reel-to-reel and cassette decks, is available in several performance grades. These are described by different terms, such as low-noise/high-output, ferric, chrome, ferrichrome, and so on. These terms refer to the composition of the magnetic coating on the tape. It has been found that chromium dioxide, when blended with ferric oxide in various proportions, will improve tape performance in certain respects, especially high-frequency response; this applies particularly to cassette tapes. In addition to oxide coatings, metal-particle tapes will be available soon. There is no advantage to using a higher grade of tape than a particular machine can be biased for, and therefore manufacturers' recommendations should be followed.

Among tape brands, the following may be mentioned as reliable and of good quality: Ampex, Scotch (3M), TDK, BASF, and Maxell. Most of these manufacturers make both reel-to-reel and cassette tape. Where long-term storage is contemplated, the chlorine content of any tape to be purchased in quantity should be checked.

Noise-Reduction Equipment

From the inception of magnetic tape recording, a major problem with the medium has been a particular form of noise called *tape hiss*. This noise is perceived as a high-pitched whispering or hissing sound particularly conspicuous on quiet passages. It is present to greater or lesser degree on all nonprocessed tapes. While tape hiss has been reduced by recording at high speed and half-track, it has remained a problem. The result has been particularly unfortunate for sound archives where storage tapes have been prepared containing an audible signal (hiss) not present on the original.

In recent years, two technologies have been developed to reduce or eliminate tape hiss. These are the Dolby and **dbx** processes. Both Dolby and **dbx** systems involve coding the audio signal during recording and decoding it during playback in such a way as to circumvent hiss production. Dolby was the first such process to gain popular acceptance. The Dolby noise reduction is used in most cassette recorders today to bring down the unacceptably high levels of hiss associated with slow speed, narrow-track cassette recording. Dolby noise-reduction equipment is made under license by a number of manufacturers, including TEAC, Sony, and Advent, for attachment to existing reel-to-reel recorders. The use of the Dolby process will significantly lower tape hiss.

The **dbx** process, employing a more sophisticated circuitry, totally eliminates tape hiss. **Dbx** equipment is manufactured directly by **dbx** and is available in consumer and semiprofessional models as well as professional (professional Dolby equipment is made by Dolby). The **dbx** 120 series is for the consumer market, while the 150 is semiprofessional. The ability of the **dbx** process to eliminate completely tape hiss is important not only when making storage tapes, but also when dubbing from one tape to another. In dubbing tapes, the hiss of the first tape is always added to the hiss of the next. If two or more generations of tapes are produced, there will be a serious hiss buildup. The use of the **dbx** process will allow many generations of tapes to be made with only a slight buildup of hiss.

Noise-reduction equipment, despite its advantages, is not widely used in sound archives. Sound archivists must plan on long-range storage and retrieval of sonic information. Both Dolby and **dbx** employ proprietary circuitry, the use of which is controlled by these firms. Should tapes be encoded with these systems, and should the companies subsequently go out of business, it is conceivable that equipment would not be available to decode them. This has been the reasoning of some sound archivists for not using noise-reduction equipment. It represents a conservative point of view. When the advantages of hiss-free recording are weighed against possible risks, many will choose to use noise-reduction. Future risk can be minimized if complete technical descriptions of the noise-reduction system employed are kept on file. That would enable equipment to be repaired or rebuilt if necessary. (It is wise to keep technical descriptions of all equipment used in a sound archives on file.) Tape hiss will be significantly reduced by tape recorders using metal-particle tape (e.g., Tandberg 20A) and digital encoding. The Ampex ATR–102 at 30 IPS achieves a low hiss figure without the use of noise-reduction equipment.

Of the two systems, **dbx** is the more effective. The 150 series has been recommended by several authorities as performing in exemplary fashion without creating any audible changes in the program material.[28]

Cylinder and Wire Playback

The main difficulty facing users of cylinder and wire recordings is obtaining suitable playback equipment. Cylinder and wire playback equipment is no longer manufactured. This leaves the user with several choices. First, old equipment—now quite scarce—can be obtained and used to play the recordings. Second, modern playback equipment can be rigged up or custom-made to accommodate the various types of cylinder or wire formats. Third, old equipment can be obtained and modified with modern mechanical and electronic improvements to achieve maximum performance.

The first solution is of interest only from a historical point of

28. "Stereophile Reports," *Stereophile* 3, no. 9 (Summer 1975): 7–12.

view, particularly where cylinders are involved. Old cylinder equipment will not maintain accurate speed, tracks at high-tracking-force levels (destructive to cylinder surfaces), and cannot produce an accurate, distortion-free output. That also applies to wire-recording equipment from the 1940s and '50s. While most sound archives would want to have such equipment on hand for historical reasons, its active use in unmodified form is not realistic, if only for reasons of preservation.

Sound archives with large cylinder or wire collections are usually forced to devise their own playback equipment. That has been done with successful results in several situations.

An ingenious system for cylinder playback was set up by Sam Sanders, recording engineer at the Rodgers and Hammerstein archives. Part of the success of this system is based on the fact that the mandrel from a Dictaphone machine (the mandrel is the turning part on which the cylinder fits) will accommodate Edison cylinders (no coincidence, since the Dictaphone company was an Edison offshoot). In the Sanders arrangement, the Dictaphone mandrel is driven via a belt by a variable-speed DC motor taken from a dismantled Philips turntable. This permits the speed of the mandrel to be conveniently regulated by varying the DC voltage to the motor. Thus, flexible control is provided for cylinders recorded at different speeds. A modern moving-magnet cartridge (Stanton 500 series) is used to play the cylinder. It is mounted in a Rabco tangential tracking system. In the Rabco system, originally intended for use with discs, the cartridge moves along a track suspended over the disc—or, in this instance, the cylinder. A highly sensitive electro-mechanical feedback system inside the device allows the cartridge to track the grooves accurately regardless of their density. The entire apparatus is mounted in a wooden frame. This system is not suitable for heavy use, but is adequate for occasional taping.

At the Institute of the American Musical, Incorporated, original Edison Standard cylinder-players are used, outfitted with modern cartridges (also Stanton, although in this case the 681 series with a 1-mil stylus is used).[29]

In a recent project carried out in New Zealand, Maori music

29. Stanton Magnetics, Inc., advertisement, *Audio* 61 (January 1977): 23.

recorded on Edison wax cylinders between 1919 and 1923 was transferred to tape using an Edison Dictaphone with a modified Bang and Olufsen SP–10 cartridge. The cartridge was supplied with a spherical Pyrex glass stylus of 460 microns.[30]

Cylinders present special handling problems. Walter Welch has detailed some of these. Due to the nature of their composition— filled-wax material and inner cardboard liners—cylinders often swell, making it impossible to fit them onto a standard-diameter mandrel. In such instances, the cylinder needs to be reamed, a highly sensitive operation. At Syracuse University, where Welch is audio archivist, such work was carried out by a specialist in the engineering department. In addition, cylinders, because of the embrittling effects of hygroscopic cycling, are sensitive to heat. Even the heat of the hand can cause small fractures. Mr. Welch therefore recommends the use of gloves in handling them.[31] Although the grooves can be protected, to some extent, by a coating of Micro-Pel, they are still quite sensitive. Once successfully taped, they should be left in storage.

30. Hans Meulengracht-Madsen, "On the Transcription of Old Phonograph Wax Records," *Journal of the Audio Engineering Society* 24 (January/February 1976): 27–32.

31. Welch, "Preservation," pp. 92–93.

3

Restoration of Sound Recordings

Many forms of physical damage to sound recordings can be repaired or compensated for within the archives/library. Such damages include breakage, warping, and pitted or otherwise damaged and contaminated surfaces. Certain recording and manufacturing deficiencies, such as hum and artificial equalization, may also be corrected.

Cleaning is probably the most widely practiced technique for restoring discs that have suffered neglect or unsatisfactory storage conditions. Cleaning techniques have already been discussed. While cleaning will help prevent further damage to discs, it may or may not be effective in reducing surface noise, the purpose for which it is most often used. In instances where noise is due to dirt particles impacted in groove walls, cleaning will almost certainly not work. Where dirt is loose, cleaning will lower surface noise.

Surface noise on 78s may be temporarily reduced—as, for example, for dubbing—by means of wet-playing. Wet-playing has already been mentioned as a possible way of reducing noise build-up on discs. The editors of *Stereophile* magazine have suggested that it may also be used effectively to lower surface noise.[1] To accomplish that, a thin layer of distilled water and Fotoflo is spread over the surface of the disc. The disc is then played in the conventional way and taped. Background noise will be lowered. Because of the possible harmful effects of wet-playing, this technique of noise reduction should be regarded as experimental. It should not be attempted with laminated 78s, such as Columbias.

Warping is a frequently encountered problem with discs. Warp-

1. "On Tape," *Stereophile* 3, no. 10 (Autumn 1975): 39, col. 2.

Fig. 11. Discs may be de-warped by placing them between two pieces of plate glass and heating to about 135° F. Heat is applied for ten minutes.

ing is usually caused when discs are subject to high temperatures or sustained physical loads. Warping of LPs can, in most cases, be corrected by a simple procedure that takes advantage of the fact that heat and pressure, properly applied, will restore the disc to its original condition.

Equipment required for de-warping includes two heavy pieces of plate glass cut in thirteen-by-thirteen-inch squares; a heat source, such as a heat lamp, natural sunlight, or a pilot light; and a weight (a set of heavy books or volumes of an encyclopedia are adequate).

The disc to be de-warped is first cleaned, then placed between the plates of glass and heated. Heat should be applied until the disc reaches about 135 degrees Fahrenheit to 150 degrees Fahrenheit. Disc temperature, however, should not exceed 150 degrees Fahrenheit.[2] Beyond that point, damage may occur. It is difficult to judge temperature exactly. Experience with expendable discs is the best way to learn the technique. In practice, it is more likely that discs will be underheated than overheated. If a heat lamp or

2. Percy Wilson, "Care of Records," *Audio* 56 (December 1972): 30, col. 1.

Fig. 12. Heat is removed, and a set of heavy books is placed on top of the glass-disc sandwich. After twenty-four hours, the disc may be examined. The warp will usually be corrected. If not, insufficient heat was applied.

natural sunlight is used, exposure for about ten minutes should produce adequate temperature. Percy Wilson has suggested that the top of a warm stove is an ideal place, although that will usually not be convenient in an archives or a library, where the heat lamp would be easier to set up.

After the disc has reached 135 degrees Fahrenheit, it should be kept at that temperature for about ten minutes, so that it will begin to re-form. At that point, heavy weights can be put on the top piece of glass and the disc set aside for twenty-four hours. After that interval, the disc may be removed. The warp will normally be corrected. If not, it is probably because insufficient heat and/or pressure was applied. The procedure may be repeated until success is achieved. The pieces of plate glass must be clean, smooth, and perfectly flat, in order not to damage the disc further. If applied correctly, this method will not affect sound-quality of the recording. It has been recommended by a number of authorities.[3]

3. Wilson, "Care of Records," p. 30, col. 1; W. Rex Isom, "How to Prevent and Cure Record Warping," *High-Fidelity* 22 (September 1972): 53.

Fig. 13. A broken 78-RPM disc, prior to restoration using Scotch Magic tape. In this approach to restoration, the sonic content of the disc is recorded, and no attempt is made to preserve the physical object. Results are not fully satisfactory, and it should be regarded as a "better-than-nothing" measure.

De-warping works best with 45s and LPs. However, it may also be used with shellac 78s, although, with them, it may not be successful. When shellac has cured, it is difficult to re-form. The most common type of warping with shellac discs is called "dishing," in which the record becomes slightly bowl-shaped.

When discs cannot be re-formed, it is possible that they can be played (and taped) using special equipment. Certain cartridges and tone arms are known for their ability to track warped discs. The best cartridges for that purpose are the Shure V–15 Types III and IV. Superior tracking tone arms include the Rabco tangential tracking system, available on Harmon/Kardon turntables, and the Vestigal arm.

Breakage of LPs and vinyl 45s is rarely encountered. Breakage of 78s, on the other hand, is common. When a disc has not broken into many pieces, and all are available, it is possible to reassemble it using Scotch brand magic tape to hold the pieces together. The

Fig. 14. The disc pictured has been reassembled with Magic Tape applied along the break lines. The opposite side will now be recorded. When that is accomplished, the procedure will be reversed, so that the first side may be recorded. The Magic Tape must be removed as soon as possible, to prevent the spread of adhesive. It is convenient to handle the taped record with a cardboard or Kraft paper cutout of approximately the same diameter as the disc.

tape is applied to one side of the disc only and a piece of kraft paper, cut in a circle slightly larger than the diameter of the disc, is put over the disc. It can then be turned over and the untaped side played and recorded. This procedure will result in a noisy recording because of the seams in the disc surface (some of the noise may be reduced by electronic processing). When one side of the disc has been played, the same procedure should immediately be repeated for the other side. It is important for the Scotch tape not to remain on the disc any longer than necessary. Otherwise, the adhesive may leave on the first side a residue that can clog the stylus. The playing of discs taped together in this manner will stress the cartridge and stylus. This method of restoration should only be employed when it is essential to retrieve the sonic content of the recording.

Some of the most successful results in disc restoration have been accomplished by means of electronic signal processing. Electronic signal processing includes filtering—both static and dynamic, equalization, dynamic range expansion, and digital reprocessing.

The use of static (or fixed) filtering and equalization, until recently, have been the most common forms of signal processing in the restoration process. Filtering at specific frequencies, or bands of frequencies, permits the removal of objectionable components from a signal. Such components can include rumble (excessive low-frequency signal, sonic or subsonic, produced by improperly designed turntables), audible line harmonics (signals at 60 Hz and multiples of 60 Hz produced by poorly filtered recording electronics), and scratch and hiss produced by noisy disc surfaces. The use of static filtering for these purposes by commercial record manufacturers was particularly prominent during the 1950s, when many 78s were re-recorded onto long-playing discs. Static filtering is accomplished by means of a filter set. While there are legitimate uses for static filtering, particularly for the removal of unwanted low-frequency signals, the technique has often been abused. When filtering is used indiscriminately an unnatural-sounding recording will result. This is especially noticeable when filtering has been used to reduce high-frequency noise components such as scratches, crackle, hiss, and so on. Successful filtering requires the application of good musical taste and an awareness that the benefits of lowered noise may not outweigh the consequent loss of high-frequency signal.

The use of equalization to rebalance the tonal spectrum of older recordings has the same advantages and drawbacks as filtering. Careful and limited equalization may help compensate for irregularities in frequency response, but it cannot be used to restore frequency response that was not in the original recording. It is typically the case that 78s have restricted low-frequency response. This is a limitation in the medium that must be accepted when static processing is employed. On the other hand, many 78s have far better high-frequency response than is often realized, and that should not be compromised in an attempt to suppress noise.

The development of dynamic filtering has made it possible to process signals from older or defective recordings without altering original sonic balance or introducing undesirable side effects. In dynamic filtering, the filter contour, in respect to frequency, amplitude, and time, is continuously modified by the content of the program material itself. Thus, filtering is applied only when and where it is needed. Among currently available dynamic filters may be mentioned the Phase Linear Autocorrelator, the Packburn Transient Noise Suppressor, and the Burwen and SAE noise filters.

The Phase Linear Autocorrelator (recently superseded by their Model 1000 Series Two) operates on the frequency-gate principle. The audible-frequency range is divided into a number of bands, or gates. Each gate is continuously monitored. When musical or speech information is present, the gate remains open. When noise, other "noncorrelated" information, or no signal is present, the gate closes. This system is highly effective in removing such forms of noise as tape hiss (which can be heard on many discs as well as tapes). It was not specifically designed to eliminate transient noise, such as pops or ticks, and is only partially successful in that respect. The Autocorrelator is a semiprofessional product. Its reasonable price (about $350) makes it a practical piece of equipment for the smaller archive.

The Packburn Transient Noise Suppressor (TNS) was developed primarily to reduce noise from old 78s. With the Packburn device, a stereophonic cartridge is used to play monophonic 78s. A circuit automatically selects the quieter of the two channels at any instant for reproduction. Additional circuitry acts to suppress transient impulses such as those caused by cracks, scratches, mildew, and dirt. The Packburn TNS can also be used to process stereo recordings. It operates effectively and will produce a significant reduction in noise from 78s. Users have reported varying results, depending on associated equipment. Some cartridges, such as the Shure V–15 Type III, appear to work better with the unit than others. Several major sound archives currently use the Packburn TNS. It is designed to interface with both professional and semiprofessional equipment and has a flexible control line-up. Its relatively high price ($2,000) will probably restrict its use to institutions with large 78 collections and active taping programs.

Other commercially available dynamic filters include the Burwen model 1201 Dynamic Noise Filter and the SAE 5000 Impulse Noise Reduction System. The Burwen filter, while quite effective at reducing noise, has been reported to produce some audible "pumping." Pumping occurs when a dynamic filter's operation attenuates some program material along with noise. It is heard as breathing or audible expansion and contraction of output level. Transient noise is difficult to define electronically in such a way that it is distinct from music. Consequently, it is difficult to produce equipment that will suppress only *noise*. With most dynamic filters, some signal will also be affected, although normally only at the moment a transient impulse occurs. The SAE 5000 was designed primarily to reduce noise with LPs. In that, it is only partially effective. There is no device available yet that will thoroughly reduce noise on LPs. (The Packburn firm is reportedly working on a new product specifically for this purpose.) Both the above-mentioned components are audiophile class, reasonably priced, and could be considered for noncritical applications.

Dynamic range expansion can be an effective way to improve the quality of older recordings without interfering with the tonal balance of original program material. Volume expanders have existed for many years, but only recently have developments in electronic technology made possible the design of low-distortion circuits capable of sophisticated response. The best dynamic range expander currently available is produced by **dbx,** their model 118. This device can either expand or compress dynamic range. The key to its success is the method by which it senses changes in program level—through a circuit that analyzes the energy level in the signal, rather than its peak voltage. The device can thus produce a realistic enhancement of dynamic range without pumping. As with filters, dynamic range expansion can be abused to produce artificial-sounding recordings. When used with discretion, however, substantial improvement can be made in the dynamic range of 78s, while, at the same time, noise is reduced. The **dbx** 118 is a stereo device, but can be used one channel at a time for mono. It is designed to interconnect with semiprofessional equipment. It is priced at about $200 and is a worthwhile investment for almost any archive with 78 holdings. A more elaborate version of model 118, the **dbx** model 3BX, is also available; it is considerably more expensive than model 118. It divides the frequency range into three bands, each of which is expanded separately.

The most interesting method of disc restoration practiced to

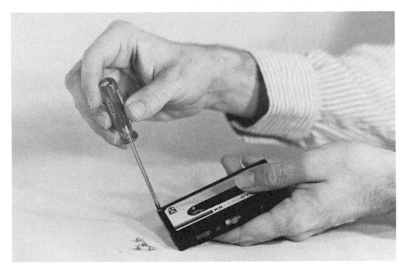

Fig. 15. Tape cassettes, especially the C180 and C120 type, often become jammed. When that occurs, it is necessary to open the cassette to make repairs. The better grades of cassettes are held closed by means of five Philips screws, which may easily be removed. Cheaper cassettes are glued together and must be broken open. In the latter case, the tape will have to be transferred to a spare cassette of the screw type, since glued types cannot be effectively put back together.

date involves the use of computer processing. This method was developed by the Soundstream Corporation, pioneers in digital tape-recording. Old Caruso recordings were enhanced using digital processing techniques. The results have been impressive. This approach at present is quite time-consuming and expensive and therefore cannot be widely applied. Rapid developments in digital processing, however, may soon make available new, more powerful and selective types of filters, dynamic range expanders, and sound-retrieval devices.

Tapes are far less susceptible to damage than discs, and damage, when it occurs, is often easy to correct. When tape breaks, for example, it can be readily spliced with little if any audible effect. Acetate-base tapes that have begun to deteriorate should be dubbed to mylar-base tape to prevent the need for restoration.

Fig. 16. When the cassette is open, tape may be rewound, unsnarled, spliced, or otherwise repaired. Kits are available as aids in splicing and in manipulating the tape spools. Handling with fingers is to some extent unavoidable, although it is not beneficial to tape surfaces. A pair of tweezers can keep direct contact with tape to a minimum.

Perhaps the most serious form of damage to older tapes occurs when the oxide layer begins to fall off. Retaping is necessary. If the tape is full-track monophonic, the Packburn TNS may be used to help compensate for the effects of dropout. It can select the quieter of two areas of the tape. Some specialty firms exist that will process badly damaged or deteriorated tapes. These have come into being mainly to service the data processing industry's computer tapes.

4

Preservation Policy

The successful preservation of a collection of sound recordings requires that a preservation and operations policy be established—either explicitly or informally—and that that policy be consistently applied to the maintenance of the collection.

With a few exceptions, most sound-recording collections are small, particularly in comparison with collections of printed books. That simplifies the creation of a workable preservation policy. Policy should evolve from an interplay between theory and practice. The feedback process can be monitored and controlled more directly when dealing with a small collection. Decision-making there will take place in a context in which implications are more immediately evident. Most sound recordings offer excellent prospects for long-range preservation, far better than printed materials. The management of such collections can be made effective with a relatively small expenditure of time.

Policy formation usually begins with the establishment of priorities in relation to available funding and the mission of the organization. Where an organization is engaged primarily in collection-building, the emphasis in preservation will be on the provision of optimal storage conditions. Where collections are intensively used, playback procedures and facilities will have to be set up that will not erode the quality of the recordings. In some situations, such as music libraries, long-range preservation may not be a major consideration. Here, the object would be only to extend the useful life of recordings at minimal cost.

Regardless of institutional mission, provision of good storage facilities will be one of the most important considerations in any preservation program. If nothing else, proper shelving must be available. If an institution does not provide that minimum level of support, it cannot expect any return on the investment it is making in its collection. Shelving requirements have been described. Sound recordings must be shelved so that they are not physically stressed—that will normally mean vertically. In addition, all sound recordings should be stored in appropriate packaging. Packaging is relatively inexpensive. In many instances, packaging supplied with sound recordings is acceptable. Some supplementary materials may be called for. They are more than worth the extra money. As a part of proper storage, all tapes destined for long-range preservation should be stored tails-out. In the small archives, these policies should not be difficult to adhere to.

Once adequate shelving is secured, the next most important factor in storage is environmental control. Environmental control can be costly. The maintenance of appropriate temperature and humidity (70 degrees F., 50 percent R.H., plus or minus 10 percent) in some locations will require expensive equipment and large amounts of energy. Fortunately, many kinds of sound recordings will tolerate adverse conditions, even if such conditions are not ideal for long-term preservation. It must be accepted, of course, that a collection's long-range prospects are impaired when the environment is not controlled. This is particularly true where temperatures exceed 80 degrees F., which should be regarded as the maximum tolerable temperature. Of all sound-recording formats, the modern LPs will be the most resistant to adverse conditions, with 1.5-mil mylar-base tape running a distant second.

Where environment cannot be closely controlled, it is important to make certain that at least no positively destructive conditions exist. For example, excessive daily cycling in temperature must be avoided. It is better to leave heat turned off in a room in which sound recordings are stored than to have the room heat up by day and become cold at night. Also, sound recordings must not be stored next to radiators or other sources of high temperatures. These should all be matters of policy. Such measures usually cost nothing to implement and can be of significant benefit to a collection. All storage environments should be regularly vacuumed. Where limited air-conditioned space is available, it is more important to store tapes and cylinder recordings in it than discs.

When good shelving and packaging are provided and environmental conditions are kept within reasonable limits, many types of sound recordings will remain stable. Attention can then be turned to the conditions under which they are used.

Sound recordings are ordinarily played either by in-house personnel or directly by patrons. How sound recordings are to be used may constitute a major policy decision. Most libraries allow patrons to use original sound recordings directly, while some allow them to use taped copies only. In most archives, sound recordings are played for patrons by in-house personnel. The principal argument for direct patron use is that the sound recording can be played in the manner the patron desires. This includes playing particular sections only, repeating passages, and so forth. However, preservation practices cannot be effectively controlled when the public uses recordings in this manner. That is true not only because most users do not know how to play recordings correctly—and may not be inclined to do so, even if they do know—but also because of the difficulty of providing and maintaining control over the necessary paraphernalia for cleaning recordings. When patrons are to use recordings directly, particularly disc recordings, no long-range expectations can be had for the recordings. Under these conditions, the best that can be accomplished is to provide reasonably good playback equipment, which will extend the life of the discs; maintain that equipment carefully; and perhaps provide inexpensive disc-preeners and encourage their use. If patrons are helped to understand that clean discs will also sound better, the likelihood of their using preeners is greater. Little, unfortunately, can be done to prevent preeners from disappearing or to enforce any kind of use regulations in a public situation.

When it is desired that patrons be able to use sound recordings directly, an obvious means around the preservation problem is to allow patrons to play a tape copy of the recording. That way, whatever abuse occurs will affect the copy only. The most convenient tape format for patron use is the cassette. The production of cassette copies of sound recordings for patron playback may, in some instances, be in conflict with the Copyright Law of 1976.

Playback of sound recordings by in-house personnel is the only means by which preservation measures can be effectively implemented (short of taping an entire collection for public use).

When recordings are played by personnel, they can be handled and cleaned properly. For discs, proper handling and cleaning includes preening with a good-quality record brush before playing, the use of a dust-bug during playing, possible destaticizing, and over-all careful handling. It also includes never playing any disc more than once every twenty-four hours. Proper treatment may also include a taping policy whereby a disc is taped after ten playings and the tape played from that point on. For tapes, it will mean playing in a clean environment and adherence to the "tails-out" policy. When playback is by personnel, a closer watch can be kept on equipment. For example, stylus tracking force can be checked, styluses can be periodically cleaned, tape-winding tension examined, tape decks cleaned and demagnetized, and so forth. None of these measures, which will contribute to recording life, are expensive to implement. Finally, high-quality reproduction equipment can be used—providing better fidelity and longer recording life—when it is to be operated by trained personnel. The use of such equipment by the public would be out of the question because of the possibility of damage.

When in-house personnel are to operate playback equipment, and an archives or library is heavily used, a remote-listening installation may be necessary. In such an arrangement, sound-recording storage and playback facilities are in one location and listening facilities in another. Requests are transmitted to the playback facility, where recordings are handled and played. Reproduced sound is relayed to the listening facility by means of cables. Listening occurs through headphones. When tapes are used, listening facilities may be equipped with remote controls for tape decks so that patrons may determine exactly which part of the tapes they wish to listen to. Since virtually all semiprofessional and professional tape decks have remote-control capability, the provision of this feature is not complicated. Remote-listening facilities are not unusually expensive to construct and may offer important advantages.

An important policy decision in any archive or music library concerns the quality of playback and recording equipment to be obtained. It is an inescapable fact that high-fidelity, ruggedly built sound equipment is expensive. There are few high-quality, inexpensive products in this field. (Among the few exceptions to this are the Dynaco line of preamplifiers and amplifiers and the David Hafler DH–101 preamplifier.) In some situations, high-fidelity equipment will not be necessary—as, for example, in an oral history collection, where speech is the primary form of recorded information (it should be pointed out, however, that some authorities in the oral history field have deplored the generally low quality of equipment in use). Where music is involved, the best possible equipment should be purchased.

One important matter to keep in mind when purchasing equipment for an archive or library is the question of reliability. Professional-grade equipment, put out by well-established manufacturers, will almost certainly prove more reliable and durable than inexpensive, consumer-grade equipment. This will mean that there will be less down-time, as well as lower maintenance costs. Among manufacturers with a reputation for high-reliability products are Ampex (tape decks), Crown (amplifiers), McIntosh (amplifiers), Shure (cartridges), Dynaco (pre-amplifiers, amplifiers), Sony (tape decks), and Throens (turntables). Most of the other manufacturers referred to in this book make equipment that can be expected to offer excellent performance and good reliability.

In addition to reliability, the sonic performance of all equipment should be evaluated. Not all products sound the same. Which equipment is superior in that respect is a subjective question. The point is that equipment should never be purchased on recommendation or reputation alone, but should always be auditioned.

Maintenance of equipment is a question that will eventually be dealt with in any good archives or music library. Sound-recording and playback equipment requires maintenance on several levels. The first level is the kind of maintenance that is conveniently done in-house. Such maintenance includes changing styluses at regular intervals, adjusting tracking force, cleaning and demagnetizing tape heads, and so on. These tasks are part of normal operation, and, in most instances, will be performed by the personnel who use the equipment. A second type of maintenance, such as adjustment of tape-recorder equalization, bias, tape-winding tension, and so on, may be carried out in-house if qualified personnel are available, but will more than likely require the services of an outside technician. Finally, equipment will occasionally fail or be damaged and require repair. Unless an archives or library has an unusually skilled person on hand to deal with that problem, outside help will almost always be necessary.

One of the most convenient ways of obtaining outside help is by means of a service contract. Often, firms that install professional and semiprofessional equipment will offer a service contract. The advantage of a service contract is that, for a fixed annual sum, service on all equipment is guaranteed, and the administrator of an archives or library is freed to turn his or her attention to other matters. Unfortunately, service contracts do not always prove cost-effective. Several sound archives in the Untied States have had service contracts and have been disappointed with the results. A service contract for a sound laboratory and extensive playback facility may run as high as $8,000 per year (the figure in one archives). When reasonably competent personnel are available in-house to handle minor problems, and when good-quality equipment is purchased, reducing the likelihood of failure, many institutions will find themselves better off handling breakdowns on a case-by-case basis. When no one is available with minimum technical abilities, a service contract may make more sense. It is possible to shop around for contracts. Local firms may vie for the prestige of serving a sound archives or similar institution.

Most archives and music libraries will, at some point, find themselves doing substantial amounts of taping, an activity that may require certain policy decisions. For example, it should be policy in an institution to tape all sound recordings that are in unstable condition, such as cylinders, early shellac and wax discs, instantaneous recordings, wire recordings, and acetate-base tape recordings. In many situations, it will not be economically feasible to tape large holdings of these items. In that event, a decision must be made on priorities. Such a decision would involve the quality or importance of the recordings, as well as their medium. Cylinders and instantaneous recordings are the most vulnerable of this group and, other things being equal, should receive first priority. All important material contained on cassettes should eventually be dubbed to reel-to-reel. Because of the time it requires, making tapes is an expensive operation, but it is nonetheless essential, if recordings on unstable media are to be preserved.

Some help for this kind of activity is available to nonprofit organizations from foundations and from branches of local, state, and federal governments. There is a growing awareness among grantors of the value of sound recordings as part of our national cultural heritage and of the need to preserve them. Institutions deterred from taping by the cost should aggressively pursue the possibilities of public and foundation funding. Many reference works are now available that analyze the grant situation in detail. Some of these are published by the federal government itself. A useful source of information on grants is the Foundation Center, with offices in San Francisco and New York.

A problem associated with all taping of sound recordings is the question of whether it violates the Copyright Law of 1976. The law specifically states that an archives or library has the right to make one taped copy of a copyrighted sound recording for the purposes of preservation, if the archives or library has determined, after a search, that a replacement of the recording is no longer available at a reasonable price.[1] That regulation covers much of the kind of taping that takes place within an archives. It is obvious that unique recordings, such as oral history interviews and all instantaneous recordings, may be copied without the formality of a search, since no other copies can exist. For other recordings, it would be best to conduct a search, a process that could include examining the catalogues of well-known record dealers or a check in the Schwann catalogue. (A record of all searches should be kept.) If an item is not found, it may be taped.

In some instances, particularly with LPs, it will be found that a commercially available copy of a sound recording exists, perhaps in the out-of-print market. What does a library or sound archives do if it wants to make a tape of such a recording, to preserve its copy of the original? It is more convenient and less expensive to make an in-house copy than to purchase a second recording from outside sources. The production of in-house copies is clearly the most practical way to preserve frequently used sound recordings. In fact, some institutions have a policy, already referred to, of taping all discs after they have been played ten times and playing the tapes

---

1. U.S., Congress, *An Act for the General Revision of the Copyright Law, Title 17 of the United States Code, and for Other Purposes: October 19, 1976* (Washington: U.S. Gov't. Printing Office, 1976). See section #108 for archival copying provisions.

from that point on. While that is an excellent way to preserve sound recordings, it is a practice that will, from time to time, stray from the letter of the law. Sound archives and libraries might do well to de-sensitize themselves on that point. As a practical matter, what goes on in the laboratory of a sound archives will never become public knowledge. So long as no attempt is made to derive commercial advantage from the in-house taping of sound recordings, and so long as copies are not placed directly in the hands of the public for use, no serious legal problem should ever arise. Indeed, there would be little, if any, way of establishing infringement or assessing damages.

The situation is different in, for example, a music library where cassette copies of commercially available sound recordings are lent to students or others for playback. In an open situation of that sort, it is conceivable that a copyright holder could institute legal action. The expense of defending such a case would never be worth the advantage gained by making copies.

It is regrettable, but nevertheless true, that the American recording industry has been more zealous in defending and expanding the rights reposing in its sound recordings than it has been in preserving the recordings themselves. Many recordings commercially re-released on LPs from earlier discs have been obtained by companies from sound archives that had the foresight and commitment to collect the originals. That fact does not seem to have allievated industry fears vis-a-vis the library community. The Copyright Law of 1976 does not give libraries or archives necessary leeway in their attempts to preserve sound recordings. Full advantage should be taken of the law as it now exists. It is to be hoped that unreasonable restrictions will be dealt with by future judicial review.

Directory of Manufacturers and Suppliers

Acoustic Research, Inc.
10 American Drive
Norwood, Mass. 02062

Advent Corp.
195 Albany Street
Cambridge, Mass. 02139

AKG
91 McKee Drive
Mahway, N.J. 07430

All-Test Devices Corp.
150 W. Pine Street
Long Beach, N.Y. 11561

Altec Lansing International
1515 S. Manchester Street
Anaheim, Cal. 92803

American Audioport, Inc.
1407 N. Providence Road
Columbia, Mo. 65201

Ampex Corp.
401 Broadway
Redwood City, Cal. 94063

Audio Dimensions, Inc.
8898 Clairemont Mesa Boulevard
San Diego, Cal. 92123

Audio Dynamics Corp.
230 Pickett District Road
New Milford, Conn. 06776

Audio Research Corp.
2843 26th Avenue, South
Minneapolis, Minn. 55406

Audio Technica U.S., Inc.
33 Shiawassee Avenue
Fairlawn, O. 44313

Ball Corp.
345 S. High Street
Muncie, Ind. 47302

Bang and Olufsen
515 Busse Road
Elk Grove Village, Ill. 60007

BASF Systems
Crosby Drive
Bedford, Mass. 01730

Beckman Instruments, Inc.
Cedar Grove Operations
89 Commerce Road
Cedar Grove, N.J. 07009

Belford Instrument Co.
1600 S. Clinton Street
Baltimore, Md. 21224

*As this book went to press, it was learned that Dynaco, Inc., after more than two innovative and productive decades in the audio business, was closing its doors. The Dynaco product line will possibly be taken over by another manufacturer. In the meantime, Dynaco products must be sought on the used market. They will continue to offer excellent value.

Beyer
See Hammond Industries

Burwen
See KLH/Burwen Research

Certified Laboratories
P.O. Box 2493
Fort Worth, Tex. 76101

Crown International
1718 W. Mishawaka Road
Elkhart, Ind. 46514

David Hafler Co.
5817 Roosevelt Avenue
Pennsauken, N.J. 08109

DB Systems
Box 187
Jaffrey Center, N.H. 03454

dbx Inc.
71 Chapel Street
Newton, Mass. 02195

Decca
See Rocelco

Denon
See American Audioport, Inc.

Discwasher, Inc.
1407 N. Providence Road
Columbia, Mo. 65201

Dolby Laboratories
731 Sansome Street
San Francisco, Cal. 94111

Dynaco, Inc.*
P.O. Box 88
Blackwood, N.J. 08012

Elpa Marketing Industries, Inc.
New Hyde Park, N.Y. 11040

EMT
See Gotham Audio

Empire Scientific Co.
1055 Stewart Avenue
Garden City, N.Y. 11530

EPI (Epicure Products, Inc.)
1 Charles Street
Newburyport, Mass. 01950

Fisher Scientific Co.
711 Forbes Avenue
Pittsburgh, Pa. 15219
(Offices in many metropolitan
U.S. areas)

GAS (Great American Sound Co.)
20940 Lassen Street
Chatsworth, Cal. 91311

Gotham Audio
741 Washington Street
New York, N.Y. 10014

Grace
See Sumiko, Inc.

Groovac
See RI Audio

Hammond Industries
155 Michael Drive
Syosset, N.Y. 11791

Harmon/Kardon, Inc.
55 Ames Court
Plainview, N.Y. 11803

Hervic Electronics
1508 Cotner Avenue
Los Angeles, Cal. 90025

Hollinger Corp.
3810 S. Four Mile Run Drive
P.O. Box 6185
Arlington, Va. 22206

Holzer Audio Engineering Corp.
14110 Aetna Street
Van Nuys, Cal. 91401

Innovonics Inc.
503-B Vandell Way
Campbell, Cal. 95008

Keith Monks (Audio) Ltd.
42 Tiffany Place
Brooklyn, N.Y. 11231

Kenwood Electronics, Inc.
1315 E. Watsoncenter Road
Carson, Cal. 90745

KLH/Buren Research
145 University Avenue
Westwood, Mass. 02090

Koss Corp.
4129 N. Port Washington Avenue
Milwaukee, Wisc. 53212

Lencoclean
See Neosonic Corp. of America

Martel Electronics
970-A E. Orangethorpe
Anaheim, Cal. 92801

Matsushita Electric Corp. of America
Pan-Am Building
200 Park Avenue
New York, N.Y. 10017

Maxell
60 Oxford Drive
Moonachie, N.J. 07074

Micro-Pel
See Certified Laboratories

Micro Seiki
See TEAC Corporation

Nagra
19 W. 44th Street, Room 715
New York, N.Y. 10036

Nakamichi Research
220 University Avenue
Carle Place, N.Y. 11514

Neosonic Corp. of America
180 Miller Place
Hicksville, N.Y. 11801

Nortronics Co., Inc.
8101 Tenth Avenue
N. Minneapolis, Minn. 55427

Ortofon
122 Dupont Street
Plainview, N.Y. 11803

Packburn Electronics
P.O. Box 335
Dewitt, N.Y. 13214

Phase Linear
20121 48th Avenue, West
Lynwood, Wash. 98036

Pickering & Co.
101 Sunnyside Blvd.
Plainview, N.Y. 11803

Process Materials Corp.
301 Veterans Blvd.
Rutherford, N.J. 07070

Pro-Disc
See Discwasher, Inc.

Pultec
1411 Palisade Avenue
Teaneck, N.J. 07666

Rabco
See Harmon/Kardon, Inc.

R. Allen Waech Assoc.
614 N. 68th Street
Milwaukee, Wisc. 53213

Reference Monitor International Inc.
4901 Morena Blvd.
San Diego, Cal. 92117

Revox
See Studer Revox America, Inc.

RI Audio
Penryn
Cornwall
England

Rocelco
1669 Flint Road
Downsview, Ontario
Canada M3J 2J7

Rodgers/BBC
See Reference Monitor
International, Inc.

SAE, Inc. (Scientific Audio Electronics)
P.O. Box 60271
Terminal Annex
Los Angeles, Cal. 90060

Scully Recording Instruments
Dictaphone Corp.
475-A Ellis Street
Mountain View, Cal. 94043

Shure Bros.
222 Hartrey Avenue
Evanston, Ill. 60204

SONY Corp. of America
9 W. 57th Street
New York, N.Y. 10019

Soundcraftsmen
1721 Newport Circle
Santa Ana, Cal. 92705

Sound Guard
See Ball Corp.

Stanton Magnetics
Terminal Drive
Plainview, N.Y. 11803

Stax
See American Audioport, Inc.

Stellavox
See Hervic Electronics

Studer Revox America, Inc.
1819 Broadway
Nashville, Tenn. 37203

Sumiko, Inc.
P.O. Box 5046
Berkeley, Cal. 94705

Tandberg of America, Inc.
Labriola Court
Armonk, N.Y. 10504

TDK Electronics
755 Eastgate Blvd.
Garden City, N.Y. 11530

TEAC Corp.
7733 Telegraph Road
Montebello, Cal. 90640

Technics/Panasonic
See Matsushita Electric Corp. of
America

Thorens
See Elpa Marketing Industries,
Inc.

3M Corp.
Magnetic Audio/Video Products
Div.
3M Center
Saint-Paul, Minn. 55101

Uher
See Martel Electronics

UREI (United Recording Electronics Industries)
8460 San Fernando Road
Sun Valley, Cal. 91352

VWR Scientific, Inc.
P.O. Box 3200
San Francisco, Cal. 94119
(Offices in many metropolitan
U.S. areas)

Vac-O-Rec
See Vor Industries

Vestigal
See R. Allen Waech Assoc.

Vor Industries
1652 Kaiser Avenue
Irvine, Cal. 92705

Watts
See Elpa Marketing Industries,
Inc.

Zerostat
See American Audioport, Inc.

Directory of Major North American Sound Archives

Archive of Traditional Music
013 Maxwell Hall
Indiana University
Bloomington, Ind. 47401

Country Music Foundation
700 16th Avenue, South
Nashville, Tenn. 37203

G. Robert Vincent Voice Library
(also referred to as National Voice Library)
Library Building
Michigan State University
East Lansing, Mich. 48824

Recorded Sound Section
Music Division
Library of Congress
Washington, D.C. 20540

Recordings Archive
Edward Johnson Music Library
University of Toronto
Toronto M5S 1A1
Ontario, Canada

Rodgers and Hammerstein Archives of Recorded Sound
Library and Museum of the Performing Arts
New York Public Library
111 Amsterdam Avenue
New York, N.Y. 10023

Stanford Archive of Recorded Sound
The Knoll
Stanford University
Stanford, Cal. 94305

Syracuse Audio Archives
(part of Syracuse University)
1009-A East Water Street
Syracuse, N.Y. 13210

Yale Collection of Historical Sound Recordings
Yale University Library
New Haven, Conn. 06520

Bibliography

Anderson, William. "Cleanliness Is Next to Noiselessness." *Stereo Review* 32 (June 1974): 6.

Brief notes on record care.

Barlow, D. A. "Indentation and Scratch Hardness of Plastics." *Journal of Engineering Materials and Technology* 95 (October 1973): 243–251.

Study of theoretical models for determining vinyl hardness. Includes results of laboratory tests. Vinyl co-polymers show considerable work-softening.

Barnes, Ken. "The Spirit of 78." *Antique Phonograph Monthly*, January 1975.

Directions for care, including washing, of early recordings. Discwasher brush and special cleaning fluid for 78s is recommended. Bans waxing of cylinders.

Berger, Karol. "The Yale Collection of Historical Sound Recordings." *Association for Recorded Sound Collections—Journal* 6:1 (1974): 13–25.

Good history of Yale's sound archives, with description of present holdings.

"Better Recordings: A Progress Report." *Stereophile* 3:11 (Winter 1975/76): 36, cols. 1–2.

Interesting article on some ins and outs of the record-making process, including the difficult question of tape-recorder calibration and equalization.

Blacker, George, and Robert Long. "How to Play Old Records on New Equipment." *High-Fidelity* 23 (April 1973): 48–57.

Consumer-oriented, but detailed, useful article on the subject. Includes a stroboscopic disc for help in determining pitch.

Blackmer, David E. "A Wide Dynamic Range Noise-Reduction System." *db* (August-September 1972), pp. 54–56.

Description of the **dbx** noise-reduction system, with good explanation of the tape-noise problem.

Bogantz, G. A., with S. K. Khanna. "Development of Compound for Quadradiscs." *Journal of the Audio Engineering Society* 23 (January-February 1975): 27–32.

Considerations in the development of a high wear-resistant vinyl compound. Much useful related information.

Bubbers, John J. "What You Can Do to Minimize Record Wear." *High-Fidelity* 22 (September 1972): 54–55.

Contains some data on tracking force as relates to record wear.

Burstein, Herman. "All about Tape Recorder Equalization." *Audio* 56 (October 1972): 26+.

Thorough explanation of tape-recorder equalization in lay terms. A good introduction to a complex subject.

Burstein, Herman. "Magnetic Shielding." *Audio* 63:4 (April 1979): 46–48.

A description of shielding techniques using iron-nickel foil and sheets in magnetic shielding. The article is mainly of academic interest, since, in most archives and libraries, elaborate shielding measures are unnecessary.

Burt, Leah S. "Chemical Technology in the Edison Recording Industry." *Journal of the Audio Engineering Society* 25 (October/November 1977): 712–717.

Interesting information on the composition of Edison's disc and cylinder compounds. Based on documentary material from the Edison National Historical Site.

Canby, Edward Tatnall. "Latter-day Gadgetry." *Audio* 55 (November 1971): 56+.

Perfunctory discussion of disc-cleaning devices, including Dust-Bug, Discwasher, Syantific Audio Cleaning Machine.

Colby, Edward. "The Stanford Archive of Recorded Sound." Brochure. Stanford, Cal.: Stanford University, 1970s?: 5 pp.

Short description of the Stanford sound archives, with some information on its history and policy. Colby was music librarian at Stanford and director of its sound archives.

Comstock, D. E., et al. "Dropout Identification and Cleaning Methods for Magnetic Tape." *Journal of the Audio Engineering Society* 22: (September 1974): 511–520.
Factors responsible for tape-performance degradation, with analysis of different rehabilitation methods.

Cook, Warren ("Blob"). "Paper and Plastic." *Record Exchanger* 3:4, 4:1, 4 and 5 (n.d. 1970s?).
Excellent four-part article on record manufacture and preservation techniques, aimed for collectors of rock-and-roll 78s and 45s. Clear explanations and specific recommendations, most of which are backed up in other sources.

Cunha, George Daniel Martin. *Conservation of Library Materials; a Manual and Bibliography on the Care, Repair and Restoration of Library Materials.* 2d ed. Metuchen, N.J.: Scarecrow Press, 1971. Vol. 1, 406 pp.
Deals mainly with printed materials. Contains some information on sound recordings, though it may possibly be misleading. References are difficult to locate.

Eilers, Delos A. "Polyester and Acetate as Magnetic Tape Backings." *Journal of the Audio Engineering Society* 17 (June 1969): 303–308.
Comparative study of the physical characteristics of acetate and polyester backings.

Fantel, Hans. "A Pampered Record Can Live to Be 100." *New York Times,* October 10, 1976, Section D, p. 26.
A survey of recent products to clean and preserve LPs. Some interesting, though undocumented, assertions on the durability of LPs.

Feldman, Leonard. "Effect of Ball Brothers' Sound Guard Lubricant on Frequency Response, Signal-to-Noise Ratio, and Harmonic Distortion Reproduced from Disc Recordings." Muncie: Ball Brothers, 1975. 36 pp.
A test of Sound Guard by a noted audio journalist at the request of the manufacturer. Feldman reports favorably.

Gelatt, Roland. *The Fabulous Phonograph.* Philadelphia: J. B. Lippincott, 1954. 320 pp.
A standard popular history of the phonograph.

Geller, Sidney B. "Erasing Myths about Magnetic Media." *Datamation* 22:3 (March 1976): 65–70.

Contains a description of the findings of a National Bureau of Standards investigation into the danger of accidental erasure of magnetic tapes. Among other things, it was found that a giant electromagnet, of the type used in wrecking yards, when placed 1.3 feet from computer tapes, failed to cause any loss of data. The gist of the NBS study is that it is virtually impossible for tapes to be accidentally erased unless they are placed directly on top of the source of a magnetic field.

Grendysa, Peter A. "Taking Care of 78s." *Record Exchanger* 4:1 (n.d.): 23.

Author describes his experiences washing 78s at the Milwaukee Public Library. Other methods of caring for 78s.

Hall, David. "Phonorecord Preservation: Notes of a Pragmatist." *Special Libraries* 62 (September 1971): 357–362.

Practical measures for record preservation.

Hall, David. "The Rodgers and Hammerstein Archives of Recorded Sound—History and Current Operation." *Association of Recorded Sound Collections—Journal* 6:2 (1974): 17–31.

Good article with useful description of a major sound archives and some of its working policies.

Happ, Larry, and Frank Karlov. "Record Warps and System Playback Performance." *Journal of the Audio Engineering Society* 24 (October 1976): 630–638.

Description of optimum design parameters of tone-arm system necessary to cope with record warps.

Hodges, Ralph. "Dealing with Dirty Discs." *Stereo Review* 32 (April 1974): 24.

Basic rules for disc care. Specific product recommendations. Warns against soap-based liquids and silicon cloths and sprays.

Hodges, Ralph. "Record Care." *Stereo Review* 28 (March 1972): 26.

Brief but good advice on record care. Explains theory of dust damage. Warns against all liquids except distilled water.

Hulko, R. L. "How Disc-masters Are Made Today." *Audio* 53 (November 1969): 26.

Good description of the mastering process, including specific pieces of equipment used.

Indiana University. Archives of Traditional Music. Folklore Institute. Brochure (n.l., n.p., n.d.).
Some information on operational policy of this important sound archives.

"Invisible Needle Could Mean No-Wear LPs." *Machine Design* 44, August 24, 1972, p. 6.
Short account of the OROS system being developed for the Navy.

Isom, W. Rex. "How to Prevent and Cure Record Warping." *High-Fidelity* 22 (September 1972): 50–53.
Useful material on warping, including a restoration technique.

Josephson, Matthew. *Edison: a Biography.* New York: McGraw-Hill, 1959. 511 pp.
Excellent biography of Edison. This is a general-interest work and does not contain much technical information on the history of the phonograph.

"Just for the Record; an Invaluable Guide for Helping You Protect, Maintain and Preserve Your Records." New Hyde Park, N.Y.: Elpa Marketing Industries, c1975. 27 pp.
Essentially a new edition of earlier publications under the authorship of Cecil E. Watts. A good account of the problems of preservation and restoration, tied in with the use of Watts products.

Key, Walter. "Keynotes." *Stereophile* 3:11 (Winter 1975/76): 29–32.
Recommends use of Water-Pik for difficult-to-clean records. Helpful description of stylus-cleaning procedure, with good trouble-shooting guide for unusual playback problems, such as low line voltage, aging components, defective plugs, etc.

Khanna, Sarwan Kumar. "Role of Polymer Science in Developing Materials for Phonograph Discs." *Journal of the Audio Engineering Society* 24 (July/August 1976): 464–469.
General discussion of polymer science and rheology (study of the deformation and flow of materials) as applied to the development of compounds for records. Article is based on work done to formulate RCA quadradisc compound. Brief section on record wear.

Leavitt, Donald L. "Recorded Sound in the Library of Congress." *Library Trends* 21 (July 1972): 53–59.
Description of the Library of Congress's sound-recording collections and how they developed. Contains some interesting historical material.

Loescher, F. A. "Record and Stylus: How Long Do They Last?" *Gramophone* 53 (June 1975): 126.

Rules for record care. Author advocates use of the wet-playing system.

Loescher, F. A., and F. H. Hirsch. "Long-Term Durability of Pickup Diamonds and Records." *Journal of the Audio Engineering Society* 22 (December 1974): 800.

Tests of the durability of diamond styluses and record grooves. Experimental results of wet-playing *vs.* dry-playing. Also tests on elliptical *vs.* spherical styluses, but no conclusions are drawn.

Lotichius, Dietrich. "Safety First—Essential in the Preservation of Sound Recordings." *Phonographic Bulletin* 5 (December 1972): 8–14.

Description of procedures and safety measures at the German National Radio Archives at Hamburg. Has information on flood control.

Maier, Bruce R. "In Search of the Perfect Record Cleanser." *High-Fidelity* 22 (September 1972): 52–55.

Discussion of contaminants affecting phonograph records and specifications of a good cleanser.

Manual of Music Librarianship. Carol June Bradley, editor. Ann Arbor: Music Library Association, 1966. 140 pp.

Contains two articles on sound recordings and associated equipment, one by Edward Colby and Keith Johnson and the other by William Shank and Lloyd Engelbrecht. Both outdated.

McWilliams, Jerry. "Storage, Care, and Preservation of Sound Recordings—a Bibliography." *Association for Recorded Sound Collections—Journal* 9:2–3 (1977): 3–10.

Extensive bibliography on the preservation of sound recordings.

Meulengracht-Madsen, Hans. "On the Transcription of Old Phonograph Wax Records." *Journal of the Audio Engineering Society* 24 (January/February 1976): 27–32.

Specific methods used in transcribing Maori cylinder recordings to tape. Technical details probably useful for constructing a cylinder-playback device.

Meyers, Alfred. "Cleaning Up Those Dirty Grooves—a Survey of Record-care Products." *Schwann-1 Record & Tape Guide* 29:12 (December 1977): A–1/A–8.

A noncritical discussion of commercially available disc-care products.

Mullin, John T. "Magnetic Recording for Original Recordings." *Journal of the Audio Engineering Society* 25 (October/November 1977): 696–701.

Excellent capsule history of magnetic recording by the man who introduced German tape recorders into the United States after World War II and was an important figure in early magnetic recording.

Odell, L. Brevoort. "The Edison Diamond Disc Phonograph—Perfect Fidelity 60 Years Ago!" *Association for Recorded Sound Collections—Journal* 6:1 (1974): 3–12.

History of the Diamond Discs and the various technical problems Edison had in perfecting them.

"On Tape." *Stereophile* (Autumn 1975): 37–39.

Wet-playing technique for reducing noise in 78s. Vestigal arm is recommended for tracking warped 78s.

The Phonograph and Sound Recording after One Hundred Years. (Centennial issue of the *Journal of the Audio Engineering Society.*) *Journal of the Audio Engineering Society* 25 (October/November, 1977).

Contains many interesting and important articles on the history of sound-recording. An invaluable item for any collection in this field.

Phonograph Record Libraries; Their Organization and Practice. Henry F. J. Currall, editor. Hamden, Conn.: Archon, 1963. 182 pp.

A good work, but outdated from the standpoint of phonorecord preservation.

Pickett, A. G., and M. M. Lemcoe. *Preservation and Storage of Sound Recordings.* Washington: Library of Congress, 1959. 74 pp.

The only major study of the subject to date. Does not include information on cylinders. Essential reading.

Pinninger, E. B. "Faults in Gramophone Records." *Gramophone* 52 (October 1974): 79.

Good description of the defects that can enter discs during the manufacturing process.

Pisha, B. V. "Record Cleaners; Do They Really Work?" *Audio* 59 (March 1975): 20–23.

Survey of record-cleaning devices with tests. Products reviewed include VacORec, Staticmaster 500, Discwasher, Watts Parastat, Audio Technica Rotary Disc Cleaner, and Record-Cleaning Kit.

Quigley, James. "78's Live!" *Audio* 53 (June 1969): 35–36.

Discussion of differing shellac surfaces and commercial dubbing techniques, especially for records for the 1930s and '40s.

Read, Oliver, and Walter L. Welch. *From Tinfoil to Stereo*. 2d ed. Indianapolis: H. W. Sams, 1976. 550 pp.

The standard American history of the phonograph. This is an exhaustive treatment of the subject. Read and Welch are particularly good at sorting out the tangled corporate history of the phonograph. Contains an excellent histogram on this subject. Coverage of recent developments is less thorough than earlier phases.

"Record-Care Products." *Audio* 62 (November 1978): 62–63.

Brief survey of some commercially available disc-care products. Description of operation, but no critical comments.

"Recovering Data on Heat-damaged Tapes." *Instrumentation Technology* 20 (December 1973): 45.

Restoration technique for tapes "curled" by excessive temperature. Technique developed by NASA.

"Retentivity." St. Paul, Minn.: 3M Company, Magnetic Audio/Visual Products Division (n.d.). 4 pp.

Good description of handling procedures for magnetic tape. Includes data on long-term storage, effects of magnetic fields, winding tension, etc. Available from 3M at no charge.

Roys, H. E. "The Coming of Stereo." *Journal of the Audio Engineering Society* 25 (October/November 1977): 824–827.

A brief description of the two competing disc stereo systems and how the industry standard was chosen.

Ryan, Edmund. "My Way to Avoid Noisy Records." *Gramophone* 51 (January 1974): 1485.

Simple article on cleaning techniques. The author notes that some record stores in England have record-cleaning machines available for customer use.

Sank, J. R. "Biradial and Spherical Stylus Performance in a Broadcast Reproducer." *Journal of the Audio Engineering Society* 18 (August 1970): 402–406.

In terms of groove wear, Sank finds a slight advantage to the biradial (elliptical) stylus when used in the RCA BDR–1 Broadcast Disc Reproducer (tone arm).

Schuursma, Rolf. "Historical Sound Archive of the Foundation for Film and Science, Utrecht." *Fontes Artis Musicae* 21 (September 1974): 128–130.

Description of the history and the contents of the archive.

Shirley, G. "Desirability of Tape-Rating System." *Journal of the Audio Engineering Society* 20 (November 1972): 761–762.

Proposal for a universal index for correct biasing requirements for tape. A reply from the A.E.S. Standards Committee notes that biasing theory is not fully developed.

"Sneak Previews—Ball Sound Guard." *The Absolute Sound* 2:8 (Summer/Fall 1976): 415–416.

Comments pro and con on Sound Guard, mostly pro. One reviewer notes that Sound Guard makes records sound better.

Stanton Magnetics, Inc. Advertisement. *Audio* 61 (January 1977): 23.

Stanton cartridges are installed in original Edison cylinder players at the Institute of the American Musical, Inc.

"Stereophile Reports." *Stereophile* 3:9 (Summer 1975): 7–12.

Detailed review of **dbx** noise-reduction equipment with comments on the Dolby system.

Stratton, John. "Crackle." *Recorded Sound* 39 (July 1970): 655.

Good article on the problem of fungal attack on 78s. Much useful information on 78s.

Tillett, George W. "A Visit to the Japan Audio Fair." *Audio* 62 (February 1978): 42–48.

A good description of the TEAC-Mitsubishi digital disc system.

Tillett, George W. "Empire Disco Film Record Cleaner." *Audio* 63:4 (April 1979): 75.

A favorable review of the Disco Film product. Contains photographs of treated and untreated discs.

Tremaine, Howard M. *Audio Cyclopedia*. 2d ed. Indianapolis: Howard W. Sams, c1969. 1,757 pp.

A standard reference work in the audio technology field. It contains some important historical information difficult to find elsewhere. The work is poorly organized and indexed.

U.S. Congress. *An Act for the General Revision of the Copyright Law, Title 17 of the United States Code, and for Other Purposes, October 19, 1976.* Washington: U.S. Government Printing Office, 1976. 90 pp.

This is the much-negotiated Copyright Law of 1976. It contains many important provisions affecting copying of sound recordings by libraries and sound archives. It bears careful study. Important sections include: 106, 107, 108, 114 and 304.

"Visit to the Small World of a Stylus." Evanston: Shure Bros., c1974. 6 pp.

Information on the tracking ability of styluses. Excellent diagram of the stylus cantilever mechanism.

Welch, Walter L. "Preservation and Restoration of Authenticity in Sound Recordings." *Library Trends* 21 (July 1972): 83–100.

A good article, covering most phases of preservation and restoration of disc recordings and cylinders. Some of Welch's suggestions may be controversial.

Whyte, Bert. "Behind the Scenes." *Audio* 62 (February 1978): 16.

Description of the TEAC-Mitsubishi digital disc system.

Whyte, Bert. "Behind the Scenes." *Audio* 62 (August 1978): 20–24.

The Audio Engineering Society's Digital Standards Committee is discussed.

Wilson, Percy. "Care of Records." *Audio* 56 (December 1972): 30–32.

Description of various record-care techniques, including an anti-warp procedure. Outlines the problems inherent in record washing.

Woodward, J. G. "The Scanning Electron Microscope—a New Tool in Disc-Recording Research." *Journal of the Audio Engineering Society* 16 (July 1968): 258–265.

A classic article, with excellent photographs of record wear caused by elliptical and spherical styluses.

Zahn, Wilfried. "Preservation and Storage of Tape Recordings." *Phonographic Bulletin* 15 (July 1976): 5–6.

Description of archival storage conditions. Discussion of print-through in terms of tape type and temperature.

Index

Acetate: as base for tapes, 50, 109–110, 116
Acetate discs. *See* Instantaneous recordings
Amplifiers, 84
Antiskate compensation, 78
Audio Groome Disco Film, 62

Berliner, Emile, 5
Bias current: correct adjustment of, 91
Burwen dynamic filter, 107–108

Carneal, Robert, 35, 69
Cartridges, 61-62, 70, 74-75
Cassettes: introduction of tape cassette format, 18–19; storage for, 50–52; cassette recorders, 95–96
Chlorine: in magnetic tape, 49
Circuits: solid state *vs.* tubed, 83
Cleaning: of cylinders, 54; of discs, 57–64; of tape heads, 89. *See also* discs
Compliance: of cartridges, 74
Copying of sound recordings, 113, 116–118
Copyright Law of 1976, 113, 117–118
Cros, Charles, 4
Cylinder recording: invented by Edison, 4; improved by Chichester A. Bell, 5; Amberol series, 7; competes with disc recording, 6–7; early problems in standardization, 7–8; Edison ceases production of cylinders, 10
Cylinders: storage of, 52–54; cleaning, 54; handling of, 100

Davis, Charles C., 13
dbx: noise-reduction systems, 97–98; dynamic range expanders, 108

Demagnetization of tape heads: 89–90
De-staticizing: of discs, 64–66
De-warping: of discs, 101–104
Digital sound recording, 20–21
Direct-to-disc recording, 14
Disc-care products, 38, 58–59
Disc-cleaning products: Groovac, 61; VacORec, 61; Decca, 62–64. *See also* Disc-washing devices
Disc-protection products, 66–68
Disc recording: developed by Emile Berliner, 5–6; competes with cylinder recording, 6–7; first wax discs, 7; early problems in standardization, 7–8; development of electrical recording, 9–10; introduction of equalization for, 10; introduction of instantaneous recording, 11; development of long-playing records, 12; introduction of Extended-Play records, 13; stereophonic recording, 13–14; quadraphonic recording, 14; direct-to-disc recording, 14; digitally encoded discs, 20
Disc-washing devices: Keith Monks, 41; Discwasher, 59–60
Discs: laminated, 8–9, 37; vinyl, 12; shelving for, 30, 33; gravity-loading of, 33–34; packaging of, 34–36; washing of, 37–41; inherent vice of 41–43; handling of, 55; cleaning of, 57–64; wet playing of, 60–61, 101; destaticizing, 64–66; dewarping of, 101–104
—broken discs: retrieving sonic content of, 104–105
—shellac discs: introduced, 6; washing of, 39; curing of, 41; cleaning of, 64
—storage of: physical positioning for, 30–34; correct temperature and

8404